The Friendly Baker

The Friendly Baker

First edition printed in 2022 in the UK

ISBN: 978-1-915538-01-7

Written by: Lucy Parr

Edited by: Katie Fisher & Phil Turner

Photography by: Paul Gregory

Food Styling: Lucy Parr & Paul Gregory

Designed by: Paul Cocker

Sales & PR: Emma Toogood & Lizzy Capps

Contributors: Lis Ellis

me:ze PUBLISHING

Published by Meze Publishing Limited
Unit 1b, 2 Kelham Square
Kelham Riverside
Sheffield S3 8SD
Web: www.mezepublishing.co.uk
Telephone: 0114 275 7709
Email: info@mezepublishing.co.uk

Printed in Great Britain by
Bell and Bain Ltd, Glasgow

Contents

AUTUMN

WINTER

Introduction

I have always loved to cook since about the age of eight when I received my Brownies baking badge after making some highly sophisticated (or so I thought at the time) fairy cakes with fluorescent yellow icing. I had experienced the joy of creating something that people wanted to eat, and I knew that was something I wanted to do again. I spent many a happy teenage hour delving into my mother's large collection of 1970s Cordon Bleu magazines, and this affiliation with Le Cordon Bleu continued when I attended the London culinary school after graduating from university. I studied both cuisine and patisserie, and more recently returned to Le Cordon Bleu to study for a certificate from the extremely innovative plant-based patisserie course. The patisserie courses were utterly inspiring, and I was fortunate enough to study under the tuition of Claire Clark MBE and Julie Walsh, both exceptional and inspirational pastry chefs. I learnt so much and my passion for food was cemented. Part of me wishes I had gone into the world of food as a career, but instead my interest and passion for cooking continued as a hobby.

It was when my eldest daughter, Sasha, was a baby and we found out that she was severely allergic to milk and eggs that my cooking was entirely turned on its head. I'm a confident, capable, and experimental cook but I was completely out of my depth as to how to cater well for my daughter. The challenge of catering for multiple allergies is massive, and I really struggled at first. You want to do the best for this little person in your care, but when there aren't many uncomplicated things you can make and even less that you can buy, it's easy to feel like you are failing. I vividly remember going to a local coffee shop with some other new mums and noticing the way they ordered a muffin or a croissant for their child without a care in the world, when my only option was some rice cakes and raisins I'd carefully brought along. Then came the start of nursery, play dates and the ensuing party invitations. With this came the inevitable stress of letting others have control over what Sasha ate, which is especially nerve-wracking when food is a potential danger. I was always sourcing, creating, and bringing safe replacements, awkwardly hanging around to prevent any mishaps, and probably standing out as being anxious and over-cautious.

I promised myself that Sasha would not miss out and that she would be able to enjoy food-based occasions and celebrations just like everyone else. This journey was compounded when my younger daughter, Sofia, was diagnosed at six months old as allergic to not just milk and eggs, but also peanuts and sesame seeds, and told to avoid all nuts. Suddenly those few items we could buy – biscuits, fresh breads, even breadsticks – were off the menu. As there were so many things my daughters had to avoid, it opened my eyes even more to how food is central to so many aspects of our culture. I became acutely aware that there are lots of situations where they might not be included and promised to try and recreate a safe alternative to any recipe so they could enjoy the same treats as everyone else. As these recipes became more numerous and successful, I started writing my blog, Lucy's Friendly Foods, to share them with others who may have been in a similar situation.

This book gathers together some of our favourites from ten years of creating friendly recipes, as well as brand new ones, and I hope it can be of help to anyone who may be facing a similar situation to ours, is cooking for someone who is following a restricted or plant-based diet, or just wants to bake in a slightly different way. All these recipes have been made and made again; I have used my classical training to ensure they're both delicious and fool-proof, and I'm sure you will find them as good, if not better, than the originals.

You might have allergies in your circle of family and friends, or maybe you want to avoid certain ingredients for health or ethical reasons; perhaps you want a few more plant-based recipes in your repertoire. It may even just be that you're looking at the budget and realising it could be cheaper to cook in a friendly way. Whatever your motivation, this recipe book will help you dip your toe into the joys of friendly bakes that are suitable for everyone to enjoy. These are all accessible recipes that will add a range of delicious, inclusive dishes to your repertoire. I have purposely focused on easy to find ingredients, uncomplicated methods, and the kind of bakes we all want to eat. Ultimately, this book is for everyone: you don't need to be actively trying to avoid certain ingredients, just looking for some tasty treats! I hope this is the start of a friendly baking journey together.

Maybe you're asking yourself why I have called this book The Friendly Baker? Originally, it came from the way people would describe food that my daughters could eat: "This is delicious, and Sasha-friendly too!" or "Is it Sofia-friendly?" We got very used to the word friendly in this context, and that was how I came to name my blog Lucy's Friendly Foods. As my recipes have evolved, however, it has become clear that this label works in several different ways.

My recipes are friendly because they are...

- Allergen-friendly, as they are designed for those with food allergies and intolerances, and open to everyone or nearly everyone (I offer guidance on substitutions to make this the case, see page 14)
- People-friendly, with the idea being that these are delicious bakes to be enjoyed by all, not just those avoiding certain ingredients
- Planet-friendly, as much as possible, because they are plant-based and therefore don't use animal products which tend to have higher environmental impacts
- Cook-friendly, since these are generally uncomplicated recipes that are easy to follow and quick to make, so even novice cooks shouldn't find them too challenging
- Pocket-friendly, because the recipes mostly use simple ingredients that are easy to source and inexpensive, and so you'll probably have many of them in your cupboards already

I've organised the recipes in this book into seasons to give you a whole year of delicious alternatives, so that every week, if you wish, you'll be able to create something wonderful to make sure everyone is welcome at your table. In each chapter, there are dishes to suit a variety of scenarios: seasonal bakes, breakfasts, sweet and savoury snacks, teatime, celebrations, and puddings. My hope is that this book will offer you something appropriate and special to bake for every occasion and guest.

Essential Ingredients for a Friendly Kitchen

This cookbook is intended to be your go-to for dipping into, finding inspiration and starting your friendly baking journey. As such, I have tried to avoid unusual ingredients, complicated techniques, difficult recipes, and specialist equipment.

Below you will find a list of the basic ingredients and kit you will need in a friendly kitchen; with these building blocks you should easily be able to make the recipes in this book. When I first started baking without certain ingredients it was hard to find what I needed. Many, many hours were spent visiting various supermarkets and health food shops to find a dairy-free cream or suitable chocolate. It is far easier now as you can buy most ingredients in larger supermarkets, local health food shops or online. If you need any help sourcing ingredients, I have listed some recommended stockists and brands at the back of this book on page 136.

Flours – I always have plain flour, self-raising and bread flour (also known as strong flour) in the pantry. Cornflour is also a very useful thickener.

Powders – Bicarbonate of soda and baking powder are essential for a good rise when baking in the absence of eggs. Make sure these are fresh as they do lose some oomph after a while. Cream of tartar is used to stabilise meringue mixtures.

Sugars – You will need a variety of sugars to make these recipes. You could potentially just use caster sugar and icing sugar, but the use of brown sugars will add to the flavour of your baked goods.

Caster sugar (superfine in the USA) is the usual sugar of choice for baking due to its fine texture which makes it easier to dissolve.

Icing sugar (confectioner's sugar) is very finely ground and usually mixed with corn starch to prevent clumping. Icing sugar is not always suitable for vegans as it can contain E341 (bone phosphate) as an anti-caking agent. Some icing sugars also contain traces of egg white due to fondant icing sugar being made on the same lines. Make sure you check the ingredients before use.

Demerara sugar has large crystals that add texture and a rich caramel flavour to the dish.

Soft brown sugar is white sugar with added cane molasses, which adds a caramel flavour and some moisture to a dish.

Muscovado sugar is like soft brown sugar but with a darker colour and more flavour.

Syrups – I tend to use golden syrup (an inverted sugar syrup) as it is readily available in the UK, however you can use these alternatives:

Honey is not vegan but gives a great flavour if you are happy eating it and is approximately 30% sweeter than sugar.

Maple syrup is plant-based and flavoursome but expensive.

Agave syrup is refined from the agave desert plant and has a much lower GI than most other sweeteners. It is sweeter than sugar, so you need less to achieve the same taste.

Butters and Margarines – When I started my friendly baking there wasn't much choice for dairy-free margarine, but the range has increased phenomenally in recent years. I would generally recommend softer margarine (usually in a tub) for creaming into batters and the harder plant-butters (in a wrapper) for any recipe that requires more fat, such as when making a richer dough, for greater stability in a buttercream, when a recipe needs the fat to be rubbed in, or if you're after a more buttery flavour.

Milks – There's a huge range of dairy-free milk now available, and it's mainly down to personal preference which one you use as they are all basically interchangeable. The only difference comes down to the residual flavour (for instance you can certainly taste the coconut in coconut milk) and whether it is suitable for heating. If you want to get technical then fat content will make a difference for mouthfeel, so full-fat versions or milks with more fat will make richer tasting products. I generally use oat milk as it's what we have in the house and it has quite a neutral flavour, but some of my recipes may use soya milk as it has better souring/curdling qualities which is useful for recipes such as soda bread.

Creams – Here too we are blessed with a huge range of plant-based creams. Do be aware of the ingredients if you are baking for allergies though, as many contain soya or coconut oil.

Yoghurts – Again, there is now a huge variety and so it comes down to personal choice. Many are made from nuts, soya and/or coconut so make sure you read the labels.

Cheese – I don't use much dairy-free cheese within these recipes, but the available range is constantly growing. You will need to do some taste testing as they vary hugely in how palatable they are, and to find out which flavours you prefer.

Nutritional yeast is very useful for giving bakes a savoury, almost 'cheesy' note.

Plant-based cream cheeses are great as an ingredient to soften a dough or make a dairy-free cheesecake.

Vegan hard cheese can add a pleasant 'cheesy' flavour to savoury dishes, especially when used in moderation.

Chocolate – It's important to be aware that vegan chocolate isn't necessarily safe for someone who is allergic to milk. This is because chocolate production lines are notoriously difficult to clean between runs, so if the vegan chocolate is made on the same line as a conventional type of chocolate, there is a high risk of cross contamination and a strong likelihood that the chocolate will not be suitable for those needing to avoid any trace of milk. Make sure you get chocolate that matches your requirements and is branded as free-from if that's what you need.

Cocoa Powder – Similar to chocolate, cocoa powder is often contaminated with traces of milk. Make sure you check your brand before use.

Custard Powder – I use custard powder as a binder and thickener in some recipes, and it also gives a good yellow colour that can replicate egg. Do check the ingredients as not all are allergen-free. If you can't find suitable custard powder, use cornflour instead. If you want a touch of yellow colour, add a small pinch of turmeric.

Kit List

Nothing professional is strictly required for my recipes but you may find the following equipment useful:

Stand mixer

Food processor and/or immersion blender

Digital scales

Digital probe thermometer

Polycarbonate chocolate moulds (these are preferable to silicone as you get a better shine on your finished chocolates)

Baking trays and cake tins: cookie sheets, 1kg/2 lb loaf tin, 2 x 20cm sandwich tins, 1 x 18cm or 20cm and 1 x 22cm or 24cm springform cake tins, cupcake or muffin tray, 1 x 30x20cm shallow tin, Bundt tin, individual pudding moulds

Cookie cutters: at least one 5cm circle, plus seasonal versions

Piping bags with one star and one plain nozzle

Non-stick baking parchment

Measuring spoons

Measuring jug

A Guide to Substituting Ingredients

A big part of friendly recipes is making them work for you and your own requirements. You may need or want to avoid certain ingredients but not others, so here's my guide to making substitutions.

Milks: Any milk can be replaced like for like. If you eat dairy, use cow's milk; if you eat and like nuts, use nut milks.

Creams: All creams are interchangeable if you stick to the following uses: double cream for whipping and single cream for pouring. To replace single cream in a recipe, use a cream with 16%+ fat and for double cream use one with 25%+ fat. If your cream has too much fat, simply dilute it with water, and if it has too little you can reduce it to give a higher fat content. The thicker part of a tin of coconut milk can be whisked up and used as a cream substitute if you can't find dairy-free varieties where you live.

Yoghurts: Like milks and creams, any variety of yoghurt can be used, it is just down to personal preference and requirement. Thicker Greek-style yoghurts are less likely to split during cooking and give a richer finish.

Butters: Any butters or margarines can be substituted for each other. If possible, stick to the recommendation used in the recipe of either margarine (less fat and more water) or butter (more fat, less water), but on the whole you can use whatever version you have on hand.

Cheeses: If you eat cheese, just replace the dairy-free version with your preferred option. If you don't like nutritional yeast, I'd recommend increasing the other flavours in the dish to add more savoury flavour.

Eggs: Replacing eggs is the most challenging part of friendly cooking, as they have so many roles in a recipe, from aerating, emulsifying and binding to adding moisture and colour. These recipes have been created to reproduce the different functions of egg, so it wouldn't be possible to add eggs into the recipes in this book. The only exception would be to use a conventional egg wash instead of the alternative given.

Nuts: If you eat nuts then many of the recipes that use chocolate chips and/or dried fruit could have nuts added instead. I often use Lotus Biscoff spread as an ingredient, so when I have used this feel free to use a nut or seed butter as an alternative if you prefer. Wowbutter (made from soya) is a great alternative if you like a more 'nutty flavour' without any nuts.

Oils: I tend to favour sunflower or olive oil, but most lightly flavoured oils can be substituted instead. I would recommend grapeseed or rapeseed oil for minimal flavour. Nut oils could be used but do be aware that they often carry a strong flavour.

Gluten and Wheat: Around one third of the recipes in this book are gluten-free, and in others you can make easy switches to make them so. I have been reliably informed that substituting a gluten-free flour blend plus a pinch of xanthan gum works well, but I have not tested the recipes myself.

Sugars: Ideally, stick to brown or white sugar as recommended because they impart different flavours.

Syrups: Any syrups can be interchanged, just be mindful of the flavour they impart. Honey and maple syrup have a strong flavour and greater sweetness so you may want to reduce the amount used.

Vanilla: All the recipes in this book use vanilla extract as it is slightly cheaper and more readily available. However, if you can find some I'd really recommend vanilla paste for an intense vanilla flavour. Use the same amount as the recipes state for extract. Alternatively, you can use the seeds scraped from a vanilla pod if you're lucky enough to have some in your pantry. Use half a pod for 1 teaspoon of extract. Avoid vanilla essence as it's more processed and made using artificial ingredients.

Free-From Key

The following icons appear on the recipes throughout this book to indicate which diets each recipe is suitable for:

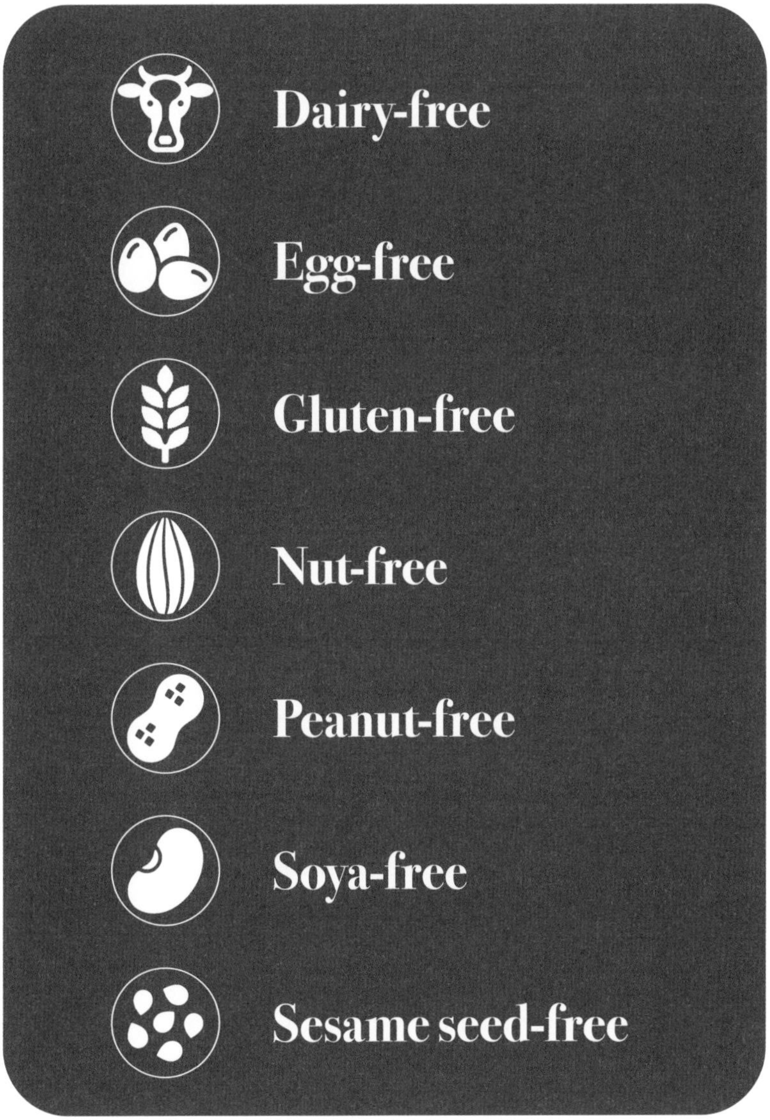

Top Tips and How To Guides

How to make your own egg-wash alternative

Egg wash makes pastries look brown, shiny, and appetising, as well as acting as a glue. To make a savoury egg wash I recommend using your milk of choice (preferably full-fat) plus a pinch of salt. For a sweet egg wash, combine 50g of milk with 50g of caster sugar in a small saucepan, bring to the boil to dissolve the sugar and then immediately remove from the heat. Cool and store covered in the fridge for up to 2 weeks.

How to make your own self-raising flour

Should you only have plain flour but need self-raising for a recipe, it's easy to make your own. Use the following ratios and you have homemade self-raising flour without needing to pop to the shops. To every 100g of plain flour, add 1 teaspoon of baking powder, then sieve to combine.

How to temper chocolate

None of the recipes in this book require you to temper chocolate and they will all work without using this process. However, you will find that the chocolate is not as shiny or snappy as it could be and will almost feel like it melts on contact with your hands (this is due to the molecular structure of chocolate). You will also need to store the finished products in the fridge. So, if you can find the time to temper the chocolate you will notice the difference and get a better finished product. It will be shiny, snappy and have a greater shelf-life. All chocolate has already been tempered when you buy it and can be re-tempered indefinitely. I would recommend the seeding method for which you will need an accurate digital probe thermometer and a bain-marie.

Finely chop the amount of chocolate you need for the recipe and place two thirds in the bowl of the bain-marie. Gently melt until you reach 45°c and the chocolate is fully liquified. Take off the heat and start to add small amounts of the remaining chopped chocolate, stirring well until each addition has fully melted and the temperature comes down to 27°c. Place the bowl back over the hot water of the bain-marie and increase the heat to 32°c. Do not let it get too hot, or you will have to start the process from scratch. Your chocolate is now fully tempered and will set with a shiny, snappy finish.

How to make a fruit coulis

A coulis is a wonderful addition to many desserts including pancakes, waffles, cakes and ice cream. Blitz and sieve any soft fruit, add 10% caster sugar and quickly bring to a rolling boil. Cool before use.

How to make a magic chocolate sauce

This is what I call magic chocolate sauce as it's quite like that one you used to be able to buy which sets on contact with cold ice cream. In a bain-marie or a microwaveable bowl, melt together 50g of chopped dark chocolate, 10g of dairy-free margarine and 1 tablespoon of golden syrup. Stir until fully combined and glossy.

How to make emergency cupcakes

When you've got virtually nothing in the larder, you'll still be able to make these wonderful little cupcakes (makes about 12 standard size or around 24 mini cupcakes). Preheat the oven to 190°c. Combine 110g of plain flour with a pinch of salt, 1½ teaspoons of baking powder and 50g of caster sugar. Pour in 150ml of water and 40ml of oil, mix well, then add half a teaspoon of vanilla extract or other flavouring if you wish. Pour the mixture into cupcake cases and bake for 10-15 minutes if they are mini, 20-25 minutes for regular. Decorate with water icing (125g of icing sugar mixed with 15ml or 1 tablespoon of water) and sprinkles.

How to make easy sweet or savoury snacky twists

All you need is a pack of ready-made puff pastry and a few additions to make a variety of easy sweet and/or savoury snacks. Choose from chocolate spread, a swipe of dairy-free margarine sprinkled with caster sugar and cinnamon, Lotus Biscoff spread or your favourite jam for the sweet versions. If you'd like savoury twists, try a thin layer of tomato purée, a scant amount of dairy-free hard cheese and some oregano, or dairy-free margarine mixed with Marmite plus dairy-free cheese if you like. Fold the pastry in half to encase the filling, cut into strips and twist into ringlets. Place well-spaced onto a lined baking sheet and bake for 20 minutes at 190°c.

How to make your bakes look professional

Piping bags are your friend for giving a great finish. They make filling paper cases or containers simple and neat, and your decorations will look professional and uniform.

SPRING

I love spring in the northern hemisphere. There's something so hopeful about the longer days and the first signs of life reappearing in the dormant trees and hedgerows. It's the sudden joy of unexpectedly warm rays of sunshine, blossom, and new-born lambs in the fields. This chapter focuses on lighter, fresher flavours after the heavier comforts of winter. We have the celebrations of Pancake Day and Easter to give us inspiration, and the opportunity to bake friendly versions of classic treats for everyone to enjoy.

Perfect Egg-Free Pancakes with Cherry Berry Compote

Roasted Banana Bread with Biscoff and Chocolate

Breakfast Cereal Cookies and Fresh Strawberry Milk

A Trio of Welsh Cakes

Chocolate Truffles Two Ways

Savoury Scones with Chive Butter

Zingy Ginger and Lime Cheesecake

Hot Cross Buns

Homemade Easter Eggs

Lemon Sherbet Drizzle Cake

American Style Chocolate and Vanilla Sandwich Cookies

Pizza Breadsticks with Marinara Dip

Super Indulgent Chocolate Cupcakes

Perfect Pancakes with Cherry Berry Compote

This pancake recipe is as simple as it gets and gives fabulous results from a few store cupboard ingredients. They have a bit more rise than traditional English pancakes or French crepes; think one step towards a big fluffy American version. These are perfect for Shrove Tuesday, as well as for a special weekend breakfast or a quick pudding.

Perfect Pancakes

Free-From:

Prep time: 35 minutes | Cooking time: 10 minutes | Makes 10-12 small or 6-8 large pancakes

120g plain flour
2 tsp baking powder
30g caster sugar
2 tbsp sunflower oil
250ml dairy-free milk

1. Sift the flour into a large bowl, then stir in the baking powder and sugar.
2. Make a well in the centre of the flour mix, then add the oil and dairy-free milk. Gradually whisk in the flour until you make a smooth batter, adding more milk as necessary to make a single cream consistency.
3. Cover the bowl and place in the fridge for at least half an hour.
4. Heat a frying pan and wipe with some flavourless oil. Pour a ladleful of batter into the centre of the pan, swirling it around to make an even circle. When you see bubbles rising to the top, it's time to flip the pancake. You want a nice even golden colour and a soft fluffy centre.
5. Eat hot topped with cherry berry compote, lemon and sugar, honey, maple syrup, chocolate spread, jam or whatever you choose.

Variations: Make these into gingerbread pancakes by using soft brown sugar and adding 1 teaspoon each of ground ginger and cinnamon. Drizzle with maple syrup just before serving.

Cherry Berry Compote

Free-From:

Prep time: 5 minutes | Cooking time: 15 minutes, plus cooling time | Serves 2

150g cherries and berries
1 tbsp lemon juice
15g (1 tbsp) sugar
½ tsp vanilla extract

1. Wash the berries and cherries. Roughly dice strawberries, leave blueberries and raspberries whole. Halve and pit the cherries.
2. Place all the ingredients in a small saucepan and bring to a boil. Reduce the temperature and simmer for 2 minutes until the softer berries have released some of their juice.
3. Let the compote cool before use. It keeps well for 3 days, covered, in the fridge and is great with granola, yoghurt or the lemon sherbet drizzle cake on page 40 as well as pancakes.

Roasted Banana Bread with Biscoff and Chocolate

Free-From:

Prep time: 30-40 minutes | Baking time: 30-40 minutes | Makes 1 x 2lb/1kg loaf

This banana bread is a cut above the rest with the addition of roasted banana, Lotus Biscoff caramelised biscuit spread, and large chunks of dark chocolate. If you prefer, use nuts or dried fruit instead of the chocolate, or even just leave it out, but do make sure you roast the bananas for that intensified banana flavour. This is beautiful served plain, but if you want a bit of pizazz then I'd recommend one of the drizzles.

2 medium bananas
1 tsp lemon juice
100ml dairy-free milk
125g plain flour
1 tsp baking powder
¾ tsp bicarbonate of soda
¼ tsp salt
85g soft brown sugar
75g Lotus Biscoff caramelised biscuit spread
2 tbsp flavourless oil
50g dark chocolate, chopped (optional)

1. Preheat the oven to 180°c. Peel and halve the bananas lengthways, then roast for 20 minutes. Mash and leave to cool.
2. Meanwhile, line or grease a 2lb/1kg loaf tin. Add the lemon juice to the milk and set aside.
3. Sift the flour, baking powder, bicarbonate of soda and salt into a large bowl. Stir in the sugar.
4. Melt the Biscoff spread and pour into the curdled milk. Add the oil and mashed bananas and stir well.
5. Now pour the wet ingredients into the dry ingredients and mix until everything is well combined. Add the chopped chocolate (if using) and stir gently to make sure it's evenly distributed.
6. Fill the prepared loaf tin with the batter and level off the top. Bake in the preheated oven for 30-40 minutes, until the top is golden and a knife comes out clean.
7. Remove the cake from the tin and leave to cool on a wire rack. Drizzle with the glaze of your choice to serve.
8. This cake is delicious finished with either of the following drizzles: 3 tbsp icing sugar + 1 tbsp water, whisked until smooth OR 3 tbsp icing sugar + 1 tbsp Lotus Biscoff spread + 1 tbsp water, whisked until smooth.

Variations: Don't have a jar of Biscoff? Use chocolate spread, nut butter or Nutella instead (if any are suitable for you).

Breakfast Cereal Cookies and Fresh Strawberry Milk

Ever thought of having a cookie for breakfast? Maybe you've been in a rush, missed your usual slot and that cookie looks especially tempting to have alongside a cup of coffee? Then these cookies are for you. Combining all the deliciousness of a chocolate chip cookie with crisp and crunchy cornflakes, you get the best of both worlds. Served with a delightfully fresh pink milk, you have the best 'milk and cookies' you could hope for.

Breakfast Cereal Cookies

Free-From:

Prep time: 15 minutes | Baking time: 15 minutes | Makes 12-14

50g cornflakes
110g dairy-free margarine
100g caster sugar
80g soft brown sugar
1 tbsp cornflour
1 tbsp dairy-free milk
1 tsp vanilla extract
225g plain flour
1 tsp baking powder
½ tsp salt
50g chocolate chips

1. Preheat the oven to 170°c or 160°c fan. Line two cookie sheets with baking paper.
2. Pour the cornflakes into a shallow bowl and set aside.
3. In another bowl, cream the margarine and sugars together until light and fluffy. Stir in the cornflour, milk and vanilla.
4. Sift the flour, baking powder and salt into the bowl and stir to make a soft but not sticky dough. Stir in the chocolate chips.
5. Roll the cookie dough into golf ball sized rounds and flatten slightly. Roll each one in the cornflakes to coat them (you will probably need to gently press the cornflakes into the dough to make sure they stick).
6. Place the cookies on the lined baking sheets, spaced well apart, and bake in the preheated oven for 15 minutes until turning slightly golden around the edges.
7. Let the cookies cool for a few minutes on the baking sheets until they've firmed up and then move to a wire rack to enjoy.
8. These will last for a few days in a sealed container but are at their best when they are fresh.

Fresh Strawberry Milk

Free-From:

Prep time: 5 minutes | Serves 2

200ml dairy-free milk
200g fresh strawberries, chopped
100g dairy-free vanilla ice cream
Up to 1 tbsp icing sugar

1. Combine all the ingredients (except the icing sugar) in a blender and blitz until smooth.
2. Taste and add the icing sugar to sweeten the milk if necessary. Blitz again.

A Trio of Welsh Cakes

Free-From:

Prep time: 15 minutes | Cooking time: 10 minutes | Makes 8-12

Each of us has an extra little celebration each year on their name's Saint Day, which offers another opportunity to bake something special. For instance, David always gets a batch of Welsh cakes on the 1st of March. These delightful little griddle cakes are a traditional treat in Wales, served for tea with a sprinkle of caster sugar or topped with butter and jam. I've given three variations that all follow the same method, so just alter the ingredients as suggested. You can pick your favourite or make all three for a super teatime spread!

Traditional Welsh Cakes

125g plain flour
½ tsp baking powder
Pinch of salt
½ tsp mixed spice
55g dairy-free butter
50g caster sugar, plus extra to finish
25g sultanas
3 tbsp dairy-free milk

Chocolate Chip Welsh Cakes

125g plain flour
½ tsp baking powder
Pinch of salt
½ tsp ground cinnamon
55g dairy-free butter
50g caster sugar, plus extra to finish
25g chocolate chips
3 tbsp dairy-free milk

Lemon and Thyme Welsh Cakes

125g plain flour
½ tsp baking powder
Pinch of salt
Zest of 1 lemon
1 tbsp finely chopped fresh thyme
55g dairy-free butter
50g caster sugar, plus extra to finish
25g sultanas (optional)
2 tbsp dairy-free milk
1 tbsp lemon juice

Method

1. Sift the flour, baking powder, salt, spice and/or flavourings into a bowl.
2. Rub in the butter with your fingertips until the mixture resembles fine breadcrumbs.
3. Stir in the sugar and dried fruit or chocolate chips. Add the milk (or milk and lemon juice) and bring together to form a slightly sticky dough.
4. Roll out on a floured work surface and then cut out shapes with a cookie cutter. Circles are traditional, but any shapes would be fine.
5. Heat a dry non-stick frying pan (or a normal frying pan wiped with a tiny bit of oil) over a medium heat.
6. When hot, add the cakes and dry fry for 2-3 minutes on either side until golden.
7. Sprinkle with caster sugar and serve straightaway. To reheat the Welsh cakes, warm them in an oven or microwave.

Chocolate Truffles Two Ways

These truffles will soon become your go-to fancy chocolate treat. They are rich, creamy, soft and very moreish. Super easy and fun to make, from a few ingredients you end up with luxury homemade chocolates that are perfect for gifts, Valentine's Day or simply a superior treat. For gluten-free dark chocolate truffles, check the ingredients of your chocolate and cream to make sure they match your requirements.

Dark Chocolate Truffles

Free-From:

Prep time: 10 minutes | Chilling time: 1-2 hours | Makes 12

100g dairy-free dark chocolate, chopped
30g (2 tbsp) dairy-free cream
20g golden syrup
Pinch of salt

To roll the truffles in:

Sifted cocoa powder, sifted icing sugar, desiccated coconut, chocolate vermicelli, sprinkles, or chopped nuts if you can tolerate them

1. Melt the chocolate, cream, syrup and salt together in a microwave or over a bain-marie. Stir until smooth.
2. Place the bowl in the fridge for the ganache to fully set but still be pliable. This will take an hour or two.
3. With very cold hands (run them under the cold tap if necessary) scoop out teaspoons of the chilled ganache and roll into balls.
4. Roll each truffle in your chosen finish until nicely covered and store, covered, at room temperature or in the fridge.

Creamy Biscoff Truffles

Free-From:

Prep time: 10 minutes | Chilling time: 1-2 hours | Makes 12

110g dairy-free dark chocolate
2 tbsp dairy-free cream
1 tbsp golden or maple syrup
1 tbsp Lotus Biscoff spread
6 Lotus Biscoff biscuits, crushed

1. Melt the chocolate, cream, syrup and Biscoff spread together in a microwave or over a bain-marie. Stir until silky and glossy with no lumps.
2. Leave in the fridge for at least half an hour to partially set. Meanwhile, pour the crushed biscuits into a shallow bowl.
3. Roll the chilled truffle mixture into grape-sized balls and then coat in the biscuit crumbs. Keep covered at room temperature or in the fridge.

Savoury Scones with Chive Butter

Prep time: 15 minutes | Baking time: 15 minutes | Makes 10 x 5cm scones

Free-From:

These scones are deliciously savoury, perked up with Marmite, nutritional yeast and herbs. They're my version of a cheese scone; something to fill hungry tummies after school, to serve alongside a steaming bowl of soup or with a simple lunch. Scones are best eaten fresh, but they also freeze well. Just defrost and pop into a medium oven for 5 minutes before eating.

200g plain flour
1½ tsp baking powder, levelled off
1 tsp dried oregano
1 tbsp nutritional yeast
40g dairy-free butter, fridge cold
120ml dairy-free milk
1 tbsp Marmite, mixed with 1 tbsp boiling water

For the glaze

1 tsp Marmite
1 tsp boiling water
1 tbsp dairy-free milk

1. Preheat the oven to 200°c. Oil and flour a baking sheet.
2. Sift the flour and baking powder into a bowl. Stir in the oregano and the nutritional yeast.
3. Rub in the butter with your fingertips until the mixture resembles fine breadcrumbs.
4. Pour in the dairy-free milk and Marmite paste. Bring together to form a soft and sticky dough. It's helpful to use a blunt knife for this part to have a delicate touch.
5. Turn out and very lightly knead the mixture until you have a uniform dough. A light touch is essential for light and fluffy scones.
6. Press out the dough to a depth of 5cm and then cut out circles with a well-floured 5cm cookie cutter.
7. Place the scones on the baking sheet. Mix the Marmite, boiling water and dairy-free milk together to make the glaze, then carefully brush this over the tops of the scones.
8. Bake in the preheated oven for 15 minutes until the scones have risen and are golden.
9. Cool on a wire rack.

Variations: Don't like Marmite? Can't find nutritional yeast? Try replacing them with finely chopped herbs: chives and parsley go nicely together, or rosemary and thyme.

Chive Butter

Prep time: 5 minutes | Makes enough for 10 scones

Free-From:

50g dairy-free butter or margarine
Small bunch of chives, finely chopped (approx. 1 tsp)
Generous grind of black pepper
Large pinch of salt

1. Whip the ingredients together until they are light and fluffy.
2. Taste and add more seasoning if required.
3. Keep in the fridge until ready to use.

Zingy Ginger and Lime Cheesecake

Free-From:

Prep time: 15 minutes | Chilling time: 1 hour minimum | Makes 1 x 16-18cm cheesecake

This is Sasha's very favourite pudding and has become a real family staple: one of those puddings that gets wheeled out when we have guests over, and rarely lasts more than one sitting. A 'no-bake' cheesecake with a soft creamy texture, the buttery ginger biscuit base and zingy lime cheesecake layer results in a spectacular flavour combination.

140g ginger biscuits (approximately 14)
50g dairy-free margarine
300g dairy-free cream cheese (I like Oatly Creamy Spread)
1 tbsp dairy-free yoghurt
50-60g icing sugar
1 lime, zested and juiced

1. Prepare a springform or loose-bottomed cake tin by lining the base with baking parchment.
2. Crush the biscuits until they form a fine crumb. Melt the margarine and then stir in the biscuit crumbs. Press this mixture into the base of the prepared tin, then place in the fridge for 10 minutes to firm up.
3. In a food processor (or with a whisk), blend the cream cheese and yoghurt with 50g of the icing sugar, the lime zest and 1-2 tablespoons of lime juice. Make sure the mixture is smooth and well combined. Taste and add more icing sugar and/or lime juice as desired.
4. Spread the cream cheese mixture over the chilled biscuit base, level off and then place back in the fridge to firm up.
5. Once ready to serve, sprinkle over some additional lime zest and remove the cheesecake from the tin. This cheesecake is best eaten fresh but will keep for up to 2 days in the fridge.

Variations: Why not make a blueberry cheesecake? Leave out the lime zest and juice from the cheesecake layer, adding 1 teaspoon of vanilla extract instead. Make a quick sauce with 100g of blueberries, 1 tablespoon of sugar and 1 tablespoon of lemon juice. As you bring it to a boil, the berries will burst to create a saucy consistency. Cool and then pour over the cheesecake.

Hot Cross Buns

Free-From:

Prep time: 40 minutes, plus 4-5 hours proving | Baking time: 15 minutes | Makes 18

Sweet, spicy and packed full of fruit or chocolate, hot cross buns are Easter's most quintessential baked goods. These days you can buy all sorts of hot cross buns that cater for different dietary requirements, but none can compare to a fresh batch of these buns. Soft and shiny with their sugar glaze, I guarantee you won't regret making these at any time of the year.

500g strong bread flour
7g instant dried yeast
75g caster sugar
1 tsp salt
1 tsp cinnamon
2 tsp mixed spice
340ml dairy-free milk
75g dairy-free butter (the one in a wrapper rather than a tub)
75g chopped chocolate or 75g sultanas
25g dried mixed peel

1. Place the flour, yeast, sugar, salt and spices into a bowl or a tabletop mixer bowl. Add the milk and bring to a dough. Knead for 10-20 minutes until you have a lovely elastic dough.
2. Cut the butter into cubes and gradually knead into the dough. Make sure each bit is fully incorporated before adding the next bit. You should end up with a glossy elastic dough.
3. Add the chocolate or sultanas and mixed peel, making sure they're evenly distributed.
4. Cover the dough with cling film and prove in the bowl for 30 minutes.
5. Line two baking sheets with baking parchment. Knock back the dough and divide into 18 even pieces. Roll into balls and place them, spread well apart, on the baking sheets.
6. Cover and prove at room temperature for 4-5 hours until about doubled in size.
7. Preheat the oven to 160°c fan or 170°c. Make a batter for the crosses with 2 tablespoons each of flour and water, then pipe this onto the tops of the buns.
8. Bake in the preheated oven for 15 minutes until risen and golden. Remove from the oven and immediately brush the buns with a hot sugar syrup (equal parts sugar and water, briefly brought to the boil) to glaze the tops.
9. Enjoy fresh or keep loosely covered for up to 5 days. These buns also freeze well. Just defrost and place in a warm oven to heat through.

Variations: Turn these into double chocolate hot cross buns by replacing 25g of the flour with cocoa powder and using chocolate chips instead of the dried fruit.

Homemade Easter Eggs

Generally, free-from Easter eggs are not very exciting and it's easy to feel that you're missing out. These homemade versions are a great alternative to put a smile on everyone's faces at the end of an Easter egg hunt. The fondant-filled variety is a homemade 'Creme Egg' and the creamy truffle-filled ones replicate Lindor chocolates. If you make sure your chocolate is free-from, these should be suitable for most people.

Fondant-Filled 'Creme Eggs'

Free-From:

Prep time: 1 hour, plus 1 hour chilling | Makes 16 mini half eggs

250g dairy-free chocolate, tempered (see page 18 for instructions)
2 tbsp caster sugar
2 tbsp water
200g white fondant icing, grated
A few drops of yellow food colouring
¼ tsp vanilla extract

Top Tip: You can use the fondant filling to make oozy fruity or minty crèmes by adding an essence or extract of your choice instead of the vanilla.

1. Pipe the melted chocolate into the egg moulds, completely filling them, then turn over and let the excess drip out to leave a thin, even coating. Reserve the leftover chocolate and leave the coated moulds to set.
2. Meanwhile, melt the sugar in the water. Split the grated fondant into two bowls, 175g in one and 25g in the other. Colour the 25g with yellow food colouring. Add a dribble of sugar syrup to make a gooey texture.
3. Add the vanilla and remaining sugar syrup to the white icing and mix to the correct texture (it should be thick but gooey).
4. With a piping bag, nearly fill each half egg with the white fondant, then top with a dollop of yellow fondant, leaving a 2mm gap at the top.
5. Re-temper the leftover chocolate and use it to top the filled eggs, covering the fondant, then leave to set. The chocolates will release from the mould after 30 minutes or so in the fridge.
6. If you would like whole egg shapes, attach two halves together with a tiny blob of melted chocolate and leave to set.

Truffle Eggs

Free-From:

Prep time: 1 hour, plus 1 hour chilling | Makes 16 mini half eggs

250g dairy-free dark or milk chocolate
100g dairy-free milk chocolate
2 tbsp dairy-free milk
2 tbsp golden syrup
Pinch of salt

1. Follow the steps in the creme egg recipe for making the chocolate shells with the 250g of dairy-free dark or milk chocolate. While the shells are setting, make the truffle centre.
2. Melt the remaining milk chocolate with the dairy-free milk, golden syrup and salt in a microwave or over a bain-marie. Stir until smooth.
3. Let the truffle mixture cool fully before piping it into the chocolate coated moulds. Be sure to leave 2mm at the top so you can seal the filling with a layer of chocolate.
4. Continue with steps 7 and 8 above to finish the eggs, then decorate with a swoosh of edible glitter, gold leaf or a drizzle of contrasting chocolate.

Lemon Sherbet Drizzle Cake

Free-From:

Prep time: 15 minutes | Baking time: 30 minutes | Makes 1 x 2 lb/1kg loaf cake

What could be better than a light lemon sponge drizzled with a citrus sherbet syrup, creating the ultimate sweet but zippy lemon flavour and a sticky, gooey top? This cake really packs in the zing, and it's been the family favourite for many years, wheeled out for any celebration when a chocolate cake doesn't quite fit. Try it, you'll love it!

200g self-raising flour
½ tsp bicarbonate of soda
¼ tsp salt
100g caster sugar
1 unwaxed lemon, zested
150ml dairy-free milk
100ml sunflower oil
1 tsp lemon juice

For the syrup

2½ unwaxed lemons, zested and juiced (approx. 100ml)
100g icing sugar

1. Preheat the oven to 180°c. Sift the flour, bicarbonate of soda and salt into a bowl. Stir in the sugar and lemon zest.
2. In a separate bowl, combine the dairy-free milk, sunflower oil and lemon juice.
3. Make a well in the centre of the dry ingredients and pour the wet ingredients into it. Stir gently until combined into a smooth mixture.
4. Pour the batter into a lined loaf tin and bake in the preheated oven for 30 minutes (until a thin knife comes out clean).
5. While the cake is baking, make the syrup. Combine the lemon zest, juice and icing sugar in a saucepan. Bring to the boil and simmer until gorgeously syrupy.
6. When the cake is cooked, take it out of the oven but leave in the tin and stab the top all over with a knife. Evenly pour over the syrup and then leave to cool in the tin.
7. Remove the cake from the tin when cooled and dust the top with icing sugar, if desired.

Variations: Why not try an orange sherbet cake instead? Simply substitute oranges for lemons, using the zest and juice of just one orange to make the syrup.

American Style Chocolate and Vanilla Sandwich Cookies

Free-From:

Prep time: 30 minutes | Baking time: 45 minutes | Makes at least 24

This is my version of an Oreo, the American favourite that you'd serve with a glass of cold milk. It's a cookies and cream type of biscuit, where the crisp, dark, cocoa-rich biscuit contrasts wonderfully with the smooth vanilla filling. It may be relatively easy to buy this style of biscuit, but these are far tastier.

100g dairy-free butter
180g caster sugar
100ml dairy-free milk
2 tsp vanilla extract
240g plain flour
70g cocoa powder
2 tsp cornflour
¼ tsp salt
¼ tsp bicarbonate of soda

For the filling

120g dairy-free butter
½ tsp vanilla extract
350g icing sugar

1. Preheat the oven to 180°c. In a large bowl, cream the butter and sugar together until fluffy, then add the dairy-free milk and vanilla. Mix well. If it looks like it has split, stir in a tablespoon or two of flour.
2. Sift the remaining ingredients into the bowl and bring together to form a soft dough.
3. Place half the dough on a sheet of baking paper, place another sheet of baking paper on top and then roll out to 0.5cm thickness. Cut out rounds with a cookie cutter and transfer them to a lined baking sheet.
4. Bake in the preheated oven for 12-15 minutes. Cool on the tray for 5 minutes before moving to a wire rack. Repeat these two steps with the remaining dough until it's all used up.
5. Meanwhile, make the filling. Whisk the dairy-free butter with the vanilla, then add the icing sugar in three batches until fully incorporated. You want to end up with a very stiff paste.
6. Roll the paste into balls the size of large grapes. Place a ball between two of the cooled biscuits and squish gently to flatten evenly.
7. Repeat with all the filling and biscuits to make your sandwich cookies.

Variations: Why not try chocolate and peppermint sandwich cookies by adding half a teaspoon of peppermint essence to the filling instead of the vanilla.

Pizza Breadsticks with Marinara Dip

Breadsticks make such a great snack, and these pizza breadsticks make an excellent friendly option. We particularly like them with a marinara dip, which also makes a fantastic and reliable smooth pasta or pizza sauce. You can either make 12 bigger, softer breadsticks, or 24 smaller, crispier ones: simply make twice as many from the dough for the crunchier versions – the choice is yours!

Pizza Breadsticks

Free-From:

Prep time: 90 minutes (including proving) | Cooking time: 10-15 minutes | Makes 12 large or 24 small breadsticks

250g strong white bread flour
½ tbsp fast-action dried yeast
2 tsp salt
150ml tepid water
4 tbsp extra virgin olive oil
2 tbsp tomato purée (if you can find sun-dried tomato purée, all the better)
1 tsp dried oregano
½ tsp garlic powder
1 tbsp dairy-free parmesan alternative (optional)

1. Sift the flour into a large bowl. Stir in the yeast and 1 teaspoon of the salt. Make a well in the middle, then pour in the water and 1 tablespoon of the olive oil.
2. Mix until it comes together to form a dough. Knead until smooth and the dough springs back when you press it.
3. Place in a bowl, cover with cling film and leave to rise for about 1 hour.
4. Line two baking sheets with baking parchment. In a small bowl, mix the remaining olive oil and salt with the tomato purée, oregano and garlic powder. Set aside.
5. Once the dough has risen, take it out of the bowl and knock back the dough. Knead for a couple of minutes.
6. Divide the dough into 12 or 24 even pieces. Roll out each piece into a thin sausage shape and place on the parchment lined baking sheet. They don't have to be perfect!
7. Brush the breadsticks with the tomato purée mix. For plain breadsticks, just use oil and salt instead. If you like, sprinkle them with the parmesan alternative.
8. Cover lightly with a clean tea towel and leave to rise for about half an hour. Meanwhile, preheat the oven to 200°c.
9. Bake the breadsticks for 10-15 minutes until they're turning golden and sound hollow when tapped. Leave to cool on a wire rack. These are best eaten fresh.

Marinara Dip

Free-From:

Prep time: 5 minutes | Cooking time: 15 minutes | Serves 4 as a pasta/pizza sauce plus enough for a dip

1 tbsp olive oil
1 clove of garlic, crushed
1 carton of passata
1 tsp balsamic vinegar
1 tsp oregano
½ tsp sugar
½ tsp salt

1. Heat the oil in a large pan, then add the garlic and stir until it becomes fragrant.
2. Add the passata, balsamic, oregano, sugar and salt. Reduce to a simmer.
3. Simmer for 10 minutes until you have a lovely smooth sauce.

Super Indulgent Chocolate Cupcakes

Free-From:

Prep time: 25 minutes | Baking time: 18-20 minutes | Makes 6-8

Chocolate cakes have always been Sofia's favourites, so I've had plenty of practice in perfecting these and making them the very best they could be. The deeply chocolatey but light and fluffy sponge topped with a rich and intense chocolate buttercream makes these cupcakes very hard to resist!

150ml dairy-free milk
1 tsp lemon juice
1 tsp vanilla extract (optional)
½ tsp bicarbonate of soda
140g self-raising flour
3 tbsp cocoa powder
Pinch of salt
100g caster sugar
60g dairy-free margarine

1. Preheat the oven to 180°c and line a cupcake tin with paper cases.
2. In a jug, combine the milk, lemon juice, vanilla (if using) and bicarb. Set aside.
3. In a large bowl, combine the flour, cocoa powder and salt. Stir in the sugar.
4. Melt the margarine, pour into the milk mixture and give it a good stir. Pour the wet ingredients into the dry ingredients and mix to form a smooth batter.
5. Fill each cupcake case two thirds full, then bake for 18-20 minutes until risen and a thin knife comes out clean.
6. Remove the cupcakes from the tin and cool on a wire rack.

Chocolate Buttercream

Free-From:

Prep time: 5 minutes | Makes enough to generously cover 6-8 cupcakes

75g dairy-free margarine
250g icing sugar
2 tbsp cocoa powder
½ tbsp dairy-free milk

1. Whisk the margarine until light and fluffy.
2. Add the icing sugar, cocoa powder and dairy-free milk to the margarine and whisk until you have a light buttercream.
3. Pipe or spread a generous amount onto each cooled cupcake.

Top Tip: Don't have a piping bag? Don't worry, just thickly spread the icing onto the cupcake and then dunk into a bowl of sprinkles.

2008 Elite Gift Boxes, UK

SUMMER

This is the season we all wait for through the long cold winter months. With abundant colour, warmth and longer days, there's the desire to make the most of it by socialising and enjoying the great outdoors. This chapter will accompany you through the summer months, featuring lighter recipes and fresher flavours. Dip in to find recipes suitable for picnics, garden parties, beach days, or even to pack in your suitcase for the perfect holiday treats.

Lemon and Blueberry Yo-Yo Biscuits

Free-From:

Prep time: 30 minutes | Baking time: 12 minutes | Makes 10 sandwich biscuits

These yo-yo biscuits are sometimes known as melting moments, which gives you an idea of their texture: wonderfully soft and crumbly. When combined with the sweet fruity cream filling it makes for a fantastic combination. These are filled cookies made for summer days, and they travel happily, making them the obvious choice for all your outdoor adventures.

150g dairy-free margarine
65g icing sugar, sifted
1 lemon, zested
175g plain flour
55g custard powder or cornflour
Pinch of salt

1. Preheat the oven to 180°c or 170°c fan and line two baking sheets with baking parchment.
2. Beat the margarine, sugar, and lemon zest together until light and fluffy.
3. Sift in the flour, custard powder or cornflour, and salt. Mix to form a very soft but not sticky dough.
4. Shape the dough into an even number of large marble-sized balls and place on the baking sheets. Flatten each one with the back of a fork to create deep grooves.
5. Bake for 12 minutes, then cool on the baking sheet for a couple of minutes before moving to a wire rack.
6. Once completely cool, sandwich the biscuits together with the blueberry cream.

Blueberry Cream

Free-From:

Prep time: 10 minutes | Cooking time: 10 minutes

100g blueberries
2 tbsp caster sugar
1 tsp lemon juice
60g dairy-free margarine
200g icing sugar, sifted

1. First, make a blueberry coulis by cooking down the blueberries with the caster sugar and lemon juice until they have burst, and the mix is saucy. Sieve the coulis to make a luscious, smooth, sweet sauce.
2. Whisk the margarine with the icing sugar and 1 tablespoon of your blueberry sauce until it is all incorporated. Place in the fridge to firm up before using.
3. Use the remaining blueberry coulis for ice cream, pancakes, or fruit salad.

Variation: Why not make raspberry ripple yo-yos by using raspberry purée instead of the blueberry coulis to make a cream, sandwiched between vanilla cookies.

Chocolate Tiffin Mousse Cake

Free-From:

Prep time: 25 minutes | Chilling time: 1 hour | Serves 8

The idea behind this recipe is that it is a decadent pudding worthy of celebrations, but it can be made relatively easily anywhere in the world. It works with dairy-free or conventional cream, any chocolate you choose, and can easily be made gluten-free depending on biscuit choice. In my experience you should be able to buy the six basic ingredients in almost any size of food store, even small local ones, enabling you to make a sensational pudding for everyone, anywhere.

85g dairy-free chocolate
60g dairy-free margarine or butter
2 tbsp golden syrup, honey, or maple syrup
8 biscuits (such as digestives, ginger nuts, or rich tea)
250ml dairy-free double or whipping cream
150g dairy-free dark chocolate or 175g dairy-free milk chocolate

1. Line the base of an 18-20cm springform cake tin or place a cake ring onto some baking paper on a baking sheet.
2. Melt the 85g of chocolate with the margarine and syrup in a microwave or bain-marie.
3. Roughly break up the biscuits and add them to the chocolate mixture. Stir well so they are completely covered. Press into the base of the cake tin and place in the fridge to set.
4. Whip the cream until it forms soft peaks. In a microwave or a bain-marie, melt the remaining chocolate (to 45°c if using a thermometer).
5. Whisk one third of the whipped cream into the chocolate to equalise the textures, then gently fold in the rest of the cream until well combined.
6. Pour the chocolate mousse mixture onto the biscuit base and level off the top.
7. Place in the fridge to set.
8. Remove from the tin and decorate as desired. Chocolate shavings in a pattern make a nice design. Once decorated, keep in the fridge until serving.

Crunchy Munchy Granola and Mixed Berry Smoothie

Here we have a wonderfully tasty, toasty oat mixture that can be adapted to your preference. Add whatever you wish: toasted seeds, dried fruit, nuts, coconut, chocolate... make your own ideal breakfast cereal! You can easily make this granola gluten-free by using 100% gluten-free oats. The mixed berry smoothie is great for a filling and healthy addition to breakfast but is also equally good whenever you want a nutritious pick-me-up.

Crunchy Munchy Granola

Free-From:

Prep time: 10 minutes | Baking time: 20 minutes | Makes 1 x 500ml jar

150g oats
2 tbsp soft brown sugar
2 tbsp sunflower oil
2 tbsp maple syrup or golden syrup
1 tsp vanilla extract
½ tsp ground cinnamon
¼ tsp salt

Optional Extras
25g pumpkin seeds
25g sunflower seeds
25g dried fruit of choice
10g freeze-dried berries
10g toasted coconut flakes
25g chocolate chips

1. Preheat the oven to 180°c. In a bowl, combine all the ingredients except the optional extras. If using seeds, add them now so they also get nice and toasty.
2. Spread the mixture evenly over a baking tray and bake for 20-25 minutes (stirring every 10 minutes) until very lightly golden. The syrup and oil will have helped it form a few clumps which add to the texture.
3. Leave the granola to cool, then stir in any dried fruit, coconut or chocolate. It keeps well in an airtight container.

Berry Smoothie

Free-From:

Prep time: 5 minutes | Serves 2

100g berries, fresh or frozen
100ml apple juice
1 small banana
3 tbsp dairy-free yoghurt

1. Blitz all the ingredients together until smooth. Serve immediately.

Soda Bread with Whipped Herby Cream Cheese

Everyone needs a good soda bread recipe. Why? Because within minutes rather than hours you can knock up a delicious fresh loaf of bread. This cheese and chive bread is extremely flavoursome, but other variations work perfectly well too, so try experimenting: herbs, caramelised onions, olives, and sun-dried tomatoes are all excellent choices. The whipped herby cream cheese is not only lovely when spread onto slices of warm soda bread, but also equally delicious on top of baked potatoes, with barbecued meat or veg, or just as a dip for tortilla chips or breadsticks.

Soda Bread

Free-From:

Prep time: 15 minutes | Baking time: 30 minutes | Makes 1 loaf

210g dairy-free milk (ideally soya)
15g white wine or cider vinegar
1 tsp Marmite
300g plain flour
20g oats (plus a few more to scatter on top)
2 tbsp chopped chives
1 tbsp nutritional yeast
1 tsp bicarbonate of soda
1 tsp cream of tartar
1 tsp dried oregano
½ tsp salt
30g dairy-free butter, chilled and cubed
40g dairy-free cheese, cubed (optional)

1. Preheat the oven to 180°c and line a baking sheet with parchment paper.
2. Pour the milk into a jug, add the vinegar and Marmite, then leave it to curdle.
3. Place all the other ingredients except the butter and cheese into a bowl or stand mixer.
4. Add the butter and rub in with your fingertips or using the paddle attachment on a stand mixer.
5. Stir the soured milk and then pour into the dry mix. Bring together to a very soft dough. Stir in the cheese cubes, if using.
6. Turn the dough out onto a floured surface and gently knead to form a smooth ball. You'll probably need a fair amount of flour for this.
7. Transfer the dough to the lined baking sheet and sprinkle over a few more oats. Cut a deep cross in the top (this will help let the carbon dioxide created by the bicarb and cream of tartar escape in a controlled fashion). Let it sit for 20 minutes, uncovered, on the worktop.
8. Place in the preheated oven and bake for 15 minutes, then reduce the temperature to 170°c and bake for a further 15 minutes until golden and crusty. Cool on a wire rack.

Whipped Herby 'Cream Cheese'

Free-From:

Prep time: 5 minutes | Serves 4 as a dip/spread

50g dairy-free cream cheese (I like Oatly Creamy Spread)
1 tsp dairy-free milk
½ clove of garlic, crushed
4 chives, finely chopped
1 tsp finely chopped parsley
A squeeze of lemon juice
A pinch of dried oregano
Salt and pepper, to taste

1. Vigorously mix all the ingredients together to make a light herby cream cheese.

Fabulous Flapjacks with Two Twists

Flapjacks are always fabulous – packed full of sweet oaty goodness and ideal for transporting on a picnic or day out. You can make these plain if you leave out the coconut and ginger in the recipes below; they will still be delicious, but the coconut and chocolate or ginger twists really elevate them to the next level. For gluten-free flapjacks make sure the oats are free from any traces of gluten.

Coconut and Chocolate Flapjacks

Free-From:

Prep time: 10 minutes | Baking time: 20 minutes | Makes about 24 flapjacks

200g dairy-free margarine or butter
200g demerara sugar
200g golden syrup
½ tsp flaky sea salt
400g oats (preferably not giant oats)
50g desiccated coconut
85g dairy-free dark chocolate

1. Preheat the oven to 180°c and line a 30 by 20cm baking tray with parchment paper.
2. Melt the dairy-free margarine, sugar, syrup, and salt together.
3. When the sugar has dissolved, mix in the oats and coconut (keeping aside 1 tablespoon of coconut for the topping).
4. Spread the mixture into the lined baking tray and bake for 20 minutes until golden.
5. Cool well before cutting into bars or squares.
6. Melt the chocolate and drizzle it over the flapjacks, then sprinkle the remaining coconut over the top.

Ginger Flapjacks

Free-From:

Prep time: 10 minutes | Baking time: 20 minutes | Makes about 24

200g dairy-free margarine or butter
200g demerara sugar
200g golden syrup
½ tsp flaky sea salt
400g oats (preferably not giant oats)
1 tsp ground ginger
50g crystallised ginger, chopped

1. Preheat the oven to 180°c and line a 30 by 20cm baking tray with parchment paper.
2. Melt the dairy-free margarine, sugar, syrup, and salt together.
3. When the sugar has dissolved, mix in the oats and both types of ginger.
4. Spread the mixture into the lined baking tray and bake for 20 minutes until golden.
5. Cool well before cutting into bars or squares.

Victoria Sponge Cake with Vanilla Buttercream and Jam Filling

Free-From:

Prep time: 30 minutes | Baking time: 30 minutes | Makes 1 x 20cm or 23cm sandwich cake

Victoria sponge is surely the most traditional summertime cake in the UK. It's the very essence of English teatime, enjoyed under the shade of an apple tree on a warm summer's afternoon with tea served in dainty cups and saucers. Raspberry jam with pips will give you a more rustic finish but use seedless if you want a more refined cake, or if you happen to have royalty coming to tea!

370g self-raising flour
2 tbsp custard powder (or 2 tbsp cornflour + 1 tsp vanilla extract)
1½ tsp bicarbonate of soda
Pinch of salt
220g caster sugar
290ml dairy-free milk
100g dairy-free margarine, melted
2 tbsp dairy-free yoghurt
1 tsp vanilla extract

For the vanilla buttercream and jam filling

60g dairy-free butter
125g icing sugar
1 tbsp dairy-free milk
1 tsp vanilla extract
4 tbsp your favourite jam

1. Preheat the oven to 180°c. Grease and line two 20cm sandwich tins.
2. Sift together the flour, custard powder, bicarbonate of soda, and salt, then stir in the sugar.
3. In a jug, mix the dairy-free milk with the melted dairy-free margarine, yoghurt, and vanilla.
4. Pour the wet ingredients into the dry mix and stir gently until well combined.
5. Pour the cake mixture into the prepared tins and bake for 25-30 minutes, until a thin knife comes out clean. Leave to cool in the cake tins.

For the vanilla buttercream and jam filling

1. Make the buttercream by whisking all the ingredients except the jam together.
2. Spread or pipe the buttercream onto the sponge and top with a generous layer of jam.
3. Place the other sponge on top to sandwich the filling, then liberally dust with icing sugar.

Variation: Why not try a salted caramel Victoria sponge cake? Add 1 teaspoon of caramel essence to the buttercream, rather than vanilla. Leave out the jam and mix 2 tablespoons of Lotus Biscoff spread with 1 tablespoon of milk instead, then drizzle this over the buttercream filling.

Fill Your Own Chocolate Cookies

Free-From:

Prep time: 20 minutes, plus 30 minutes chilling | Baking time: 10 minutes | Makes 9-12 large cookies

What's better than a chocolate cookie? A chocolate cookie with a filling, of course! I've made these for years with marshmallows in the centre, like a cookie version of a s'more. Both vegan and non-vegetarian mallows work well, depending on your requirements. This recipe also works brilliantly with various other fillings: chocolate truffles (see page 30) are amazing, as is a scoop of frozen Biscoff spread, or a square of caramel-filled chocolate. All you've got to decide is what your favourite surprise filling is going to be!

115g dairy-free margarine
200g soft brown sugar
2 tbsp golden syrup
½ tsp vanilla extract
150g plain flour
30g cocoa powder
½ tsp bicarbonate of soda
¼ tsp salt

Filling Options

9-12 standard size marshmallows
9-12 tsp Lotus Biscoff spread (ideally frozen in teaspoons)
9-12 squares of caramel-filled chocolate, chilled
9-12 small chocolate truffles (see page 30)

1. Cream the margarine, sugar, syrup, and vanilla together.
2. Sift in the flour, cocoa, bicarbonate of soda and salt. Mix to a stiff but soft dough.
3. Take a tablespoon of the chocolate dough and pat out to a small flat circle. Place the filling of your choice in the middle of the circle and bring the sides up and around to form a ball. Make sure there are no gaps.
4. Place the filled cookie on a lined cookie sheet and slightly press down with the prongs of a fork. Repeat with the remaining dough and filling to make 9-12 filled cookies.
5. Place in the fridge for 30 minutes to chill. Meanwhile, preheat the oven to 180°c.
6. Bake the chilled cookies for 10 minutes. Cool for a couple more minutes on the sheet before transferring to a wire rack. These cookies keep well for a few days in a sealed container.

Sweetcorn Fritters with Spicy Tomato Relish

I've included these fritters in this book because they were one of the first recipes I ever created, and they've been on repeat ever since. Fritters make a great addition to a fried breakfast or brunch, a light and tasty lunch with a salsa and salad, or a superior filling for a vegetarian wrap. The spicy tomato relish makes a lovely, vibrant addition to these fritters but also goes perfectly with vegetarian sausages and burgers.

Sweetcorn Fritters

Free-From:

Prep time: 10 minutes | Cooking time: 15 minutes | Serves 3-4

80g plain flour
1 tbsp baking powder
¼ tsp salt
100ml water
1 small tin of sweetcorn (140g drained weight)
1-2 tbsp flavourless oil, for frying

1. Sift the dry ingredients into a bowl, then stir in the water to make a smooth but thick paste. Stir in the sweetcorn.
2. Heat 1 tablespoon of oil in a frying pan. Once hot, drop in dollops of the batter and fry until golden on both sides. Add more oil for the second batch if the pan is looking dry. Serve hot.

Variations: Use any veg you like in these fritters. Grated courgette, defrosted peas or even grated carrot are all good choices. Alternatively, try adding chopped chilli, spring onions and coriander to the sweetcorn version for extra flavour.

Spicy Tomato Relish

Free-From:

Prep time: 5 minutes | Cooking time: 10 minutes | Serves 4

2 shallots, finely chopped
1 clove of garlic, crushed
½ tbsp olive oil
100g cherry tomatoes, roughly chopped
1 tsp red wine vinegar
1 tsp sugar
½ tsp smoked paprika
1 dried chilli, crushed
Salt and pepper

1. Sauté the shallot and garlic in the olive oil until fragrant but not coloured.
2. Add the tomatoes, vinegar, sugar, smoked paprika and dried chilli. Season with a little salt and pepper, stirring everything well.
3. Simmer gently for 10 minutes until the mixture is jam-like.
4. Allow the relish to cool, then taste and adjust the seasoning if required.

Cookies and Cream Cloud Pie

Free-From:

Prep time: 20 minutes | Chilling time: 1 hour minimum | Serves 8

I'm not sure if a cloud pie is a well-known thing, but it is such a great description for this cheesecake/mousse cake mix-up. The lightly whipped cream gives a wonderfully fluffy texture to the airy cheesecake layer, and the little cookie crumbs add a hint of texture. This is the perfect chilled, delicate, light pudding for warm days. For a gluten-free version simply use suitable cream cheese, cream, and biscuits.

200g chocolate sandwich cookies
75g dairy-free margarine
250ml dairy-free double or whipping cream
150g dairy-free cream cheese
60-75g icing sugar, to taste
1½ tsp vanilla extract

1. Finely crush 150g of the sandwich cookies and melt the dairy-free margarine. Combine well in a bowl, then press into the bottom of an 18-20cm cake tin and place in the fridge to set.
2. Whip the cream until it forms soft peaks, then set aside.
3. Whisk the cream cheese with 60g of icing sugar and the vanilla until it's nice and smooth and light. Whisk in one third of the whipped cream to equalise the textures, then gently fold in the remaining whipped cream.
4. Taste the cream mixture and add the extra 15g of icing sugar if desired. Set a few spoonfuls aside and transfer the rest into a piping bag with a fluted nozzle if you wish to decorate the pie with rosettes.
5. Roughly crush the remaining sandwich cookies and stir them into the cheesecake mix. Spoon onto the chilled base and smooth over. Remove the tin and decorate with any remaining cookie crumbs and rosettes of whipped cream, or use extra cookies as decoration.
6. Place in the fridge for at least 30 minutes to set. This pie keeps in the fridge for about 3 days.

Legendary Vegetarian Sausage Rolls

Free-From:

Prep time: 20 minutes | Baking time: 20 minutes | Makes around 25

These little flaky beauties really have achieved legendary status among our friends and family. No picnic or tea is complete without a batch. People demand them: my daughters' friends say they would happily eat them all day, and this is from non-veggies! They're made with beans so have plenty of protein snuck in without taking away from their delicious taste and texture.

1 tin of pinto or borlotti beans (240g drained weight)
60g fresh breadcrumbs
½ onion, very finely chopped
1 small apple, grated
1 tbsp lemon juice
½ tbsp balsamic vinegar
½ tbsp soy sauce (or salt to taste if avoiding soya)
½ tsp smoked paprika
Salt and pepper
1 pack of ready-rolled puff pastry
Dairy-free milk

1. Preheat the oven to 200°c. Blend the drained beans in a food processor or mash them thoroughly with a potato masher.
2. Add the breadcrumbs, onion, apple, flavourings, and seasoning to the bean paste. Blitz, then taste and add more soy sauce, lemon juice or balsamic vinegar if required.
3. Roll out the puff pastry into a large rectangle and place the filling on top in a neat line about 2cm from the edge of the pastry.
4. Brush one edge of the pastry with the milk. Roll the pastry around the filling to form a sausage shape, connecting the dry pastry with the milk-brushed edge. Trim off the excess pastry to leave you with a neat roll with the seam underneath.
5. Prick the top of the roll with a knife and then cut into 5cm sausage rolls.
6. Place the sausage rolls on a baking sheet and brush with dairy-free milk.
7. Bake for 20 minutes, or until golden.
8. When cooked, cool on a wire rack. These freeze brilliantly.

Variations: If you don't want to use beans, chestnut purée makes a great alternative.

Sensational Scones with Speedy Raspberry Jam

Surely no afternoon tea is complete without a plateful of light and fluffy scones. Just make sure you have a light touch while making these and you'll end up with some super scones. Simply add some speedy raspberry jam and dairy-free whipped cream for a sensational afternoon tea at home.

Sensational Scones

Free-From:

Prep time: 15 minutes | Baking time: 15 minutes | Makes 10-12 x 5cm scones

450g plain flour
3 tsp baking powder
¼ tsp salt
70g caster sugar
75g dairy-free butter
300ml dairy-free milk
1 tsp vanilla extract (optional)
1 tbsp dairy-free milk or egg wash (see page 18)
2 tbsp crunchy sugar, such as demerara or granulated

1. Preheat the oven to 200°c. Sift the flour and baking powder into a large bowl, then stir in the salt and sugar.
2. With your fingertips, gently rub in the dairy-free butter until the mixture looks like breadcrumbs.
3. Make a well in the centre and pour in the dairy-free milk and vanilla (if using).
4. Bring together to a very soft, sticky dough. Turn onto a floured surface and very gently knead to make a soft, smooth dough.
5. Pat out with your fingers to 3cm thickness. Cut out scones with a well-floured 5cm cookie cutter (or whatever size you choose).
6. Place the scones on an oiled and floured baking sheet. Brush the tops with dairy-free milk or egg wash, then sprinkle with the demerara or granulated sugar.
7. Bake in the preheated oven for 15 minutes, until golden on top. Cool on a wire rack.

Variations: Why not try lemon drizzle scones? Replace the vanilla with the zest of a lemon, and 50ml of the milk with lemon juice. Brush the tops with lemon juice and sprinkle with granulated sugar before baking.

Speedy Raspberry Jam

Free-From:

Cooking time: 10 minutes

400g raspberries, washed
300g white sugar
1 lemon, juiced

1. Heat the raspberries in a saucepan until they start to release their juice.
2. Stir in the white sugar. Bring to a rolling boil, then simmer for about 5 minutes until the jam starts to thicken.
3. Stir in the lemon juice and store in a sterilised jar.

Popcorn Cereal Bars

Free-From:

Prep time: 25 minutes | Chilling time: 1 hour | Makes 8-10 big bars or 16-20 small bites

These evolved from a cupboard raid during the first Covid lockdown when supplies were short, and we couldn't just nip out to the shops on a whim. After much experimentation, this was the winning combination: toasty oats for a flapjack feel, cornflakes for the cereal taste and crunch, alongside popcorn for salty, sweet, chewy hits. These bars have been declared delicious and are made on repeat. I urge you to make a batch for the week ahead and hand them out to friends and colleagues.

50g oats
80g caster sugar
120g golden syrup
60g Lotus Biscoff spread
85g dairy-free dark chocolate
50g cornflakes
17g popcorn (a small bag)

1. Spread the oats onto a baking sheet and bake in the oven at 180°c for 15 minutes until toasty.
2. Melt the sugar, syrup and Biscoff spread together until you have a thick smooth mixture. Stir in 15g of the chocolate.
3. Stir the oats, cornflakes and popcorn into the syrupy mixture. Mix until everything is coated in the rich caramel sauce.
4. Press into a loaf tin lined with parchment paper. I used a 2lb loaf tin which is perfect for this quantity. If you want to make more, double the ingredients and use a standard square baking tin.
5. Place in the fridge or a cool place to set.
6. Melt the remaining 70g of chocolate and drizzle over the top, then leave to set again.
7. Cut into bars or squares to serve.

Variations: Sunflower seed butter makes a lovely alternative to the Biscoff spread.

Summer Berry Sorbet with Arlettes (Caramel Wafers)

There are so many more allergen-safe ice creams available these days, but sometimes you still can't find one that's suitable and delicious. This super easy sorbet recipe means everyone can enjoy a refreshing icy dessert, and it also easily beats the flavour of most shop-bought varieties. Served with the crispy caramel wafers, this is summer dessert heaven.

Summer Berry Sorbet

Free-From:

Prep time: 15 minutes | Freezing time: 4-5 hours | Serves 6 or more

400g summer berries
150g caster sugar
200ml water
½ lemon, juiced

1. Roughly chop the berries and then whizz up in a food blender. Sieve if you like a smooth sorbet, don't if you like some pips.
2. Dissolve the sugar in the water and lemon juice by bringing the mixture to a rolling boil. Immediately turn off the heat and stir in the berry purée.
3. Pour the mixture into an ice cream machine and churn as instructed or pour into a Tupperware box and place in the freezer. If using the Tupperware method, remove from the freezer every hour or so and give the sorbet a good stir or whisk to break up any large ice crystals. The whole process should take 4 or 5 hours.

Arlettes (Caramel Wafers)

Free-From:

Prep time: 45 minutes | Baking time: 6-10 minutes | Makes about 20

½ pack of ready-made puff pastry
Lots of icing sugar

1. Roll out the puff pastry into a neat rectangle and then roll up to form a tight cylinder. Wrap and freeze for at least 30 minutes so it is very cold.
2. Once chilled, cut the puff pastry roll into 0.5cm slices.
3. Preheat the oven to 200°c. Create a mound of icing sugar on the worktop and place a puff pastry slice on top. Roll out each circle until very thin and totally covered in the icing sugar.
4. Stamp out fluted circles or traditional leaf shapes from the circles and place carefully on a lined baking sheet.
5. Bake the wafers for 5-6 minutes until totally golden. Keep a close eye on them so they don't burn. Once golden, turn over and bake for another couple of minutes.
6. Cool on a wire rack. These are best eaten on the day they're made.

AUTUMN

Autumn: the time of harvest abundance, crisp mornings and falling leaves. It's back to school after the summer frivolities, time to start thinking about wrapping up and getting cosy. As well as recipes with seasonal ingredients, the flavour profile turns richer with more chocolate and spice. For us, Autumn is birthday season, so you'll find my knock-out chocolate birthday cake in this chapter, as well as harvest time and Bonfire Night staples.

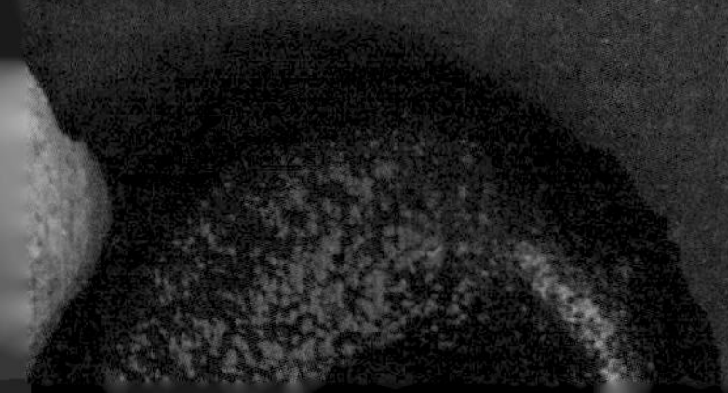

Apple Galette

Free-From:

Prep time: 10 minutes | Baking time: 20-25 minutes | Serves 6

You just have to use apples in the Autumn, don't you think? This stunningly beautiful but extremely easy tart will use up those windfalls and always impress guests. You can't get better than that! To make this gluten-free simply use gluten-free puff pastry.

½ pack of ready-made puff pastry
1-2 crisp eating apples
10g dairy-free butter, melted
2 tbsp caster sugar
Icing sugar, to finish

1. Preheat the oven to 200°c and roll out the pastry to 0.5cm thick. Use a large dinner plate (approximately 25cm diameter) as a template to cut out a perfect circle from the pastry. Transfer this to an un-greased baking sheet.
2. Quarter and core the apples (no need to peel them unless you really want to), then cut into very thin slices. Decoratively arrange the slices on the pastry circle, slightly overlapping each other in a fan shape.
3. Brush the pastry and apples with the melted butter, then evenly sprinkle the caster sugar over the top of the tart.
4. Bake in the preheated oven for 20-25 minutes, until the apples are golden on top and the pastry is cooked through.
5. Dust the tart with icing sugar and serve warm with dairy-free ice cream, custard or cream.

Variations: Make a spiced apple galette by spreading 2 tablespoons of Lotus Biscoff spread onto the pastry before adding the apples and adding half a teaspoon of cinnamon to the caster sugar.

Vanilla Fudge

Free-From:

Prep time: 30 minutes | Setting time: 1 hour | Makes about 48 little squares

It's taken me years to perfect my fudge recipe, and there's been a lot of keen taste testing along the way, but this recipe knocks the socks off others we've tried. There is a lot of stirring involved but the resulting smooth and creamy vanilla-scented fudge is well worth the effort. Make it gluten-free by using a double cream that works for you.

100g dairy-free margarine
550g demerara sugar
200g golden syrup
350ml dairy-free double cream
2 tsp vanilla extract
½ tsp flaky sea salt

1. Melt the margarine, sugar, syrup, and cream together over a low heat until all the sugar crystals have dissolved.
2. Turn up the heat and bring to a rolling boil. Heat, stirring now and then, until it reaches exactly 116°c.
3. Turn off the heat, stir in the vanilla and salt, then beat vigorously for 10-20 minutes until the fudge thickens from a liquid to a thick paste. The fudge will also lighten in colour, changing to a pale brown.
4. Pour into a baking tin lined with non-stick parchment paper and leave to set. This takes an hour or so as you want it to be fully set before attempting to cut the fudge into bite-sized cubes.

Variations: For extra extravagance, top the fudge with 50g of finely chopped dark chocolate while it's still warm and then leave to set.

Raspberry and Vanilla Pinwheel Cookies

Free-From:

Prep time: 50 minutes | Baking time: 10 minutes | Makes about 20

I hesitated about including these oh-so-pretty cookies as they involve more time and technique, but my girls Sasha and Sofia insisted I made space for them as they are personal favourites. I can see why they like them so much; they're so pretty and fun-looking, full of flavour and a bit different to other cookies. I hope they become a favourite of yours too.

250g plain flour
2 tbsp cornflour
¼ tsp salt
¼ tsp baking powder
200g dairy-free butter
180g caster sugar
1 tbsp dairy-free milk
½ tsp vanilla extract
5g or 2 tbsp freeze-dried raspberry pieces
¼ tsp natural raspberry flavouring (optional)
¼ tsp natural pink food colouring
1 tbsp sprinkles

1. Sift the flour, cornflour, salt, and baking powder together.
2. In another bowl, cream the butter, sugar, and milk together until light and fluffy. Add the flour mixture and stir well.
3. Split the dough into two equal portions. Add the vanilla to one half and set aside. Add the freeze-dried berries, raspberry flavouring (if using) and food colouring to the other half and thoroughly combine.
4. Sandwich the vanilla dough between sheets of baking paper and roll out into an even rectangular shape of approximately 0.5cm thick. Repeat with the raspberry dough. Remove the top piece of baking paper from each piece of dough and sandwich them dough side together. Starting from the long side of the rectangle, tightly roll the two layers together into a cylinder shape, using the paper to help you.
5. Remove the dough from the baking paper and scatter the sprinkles over the paper, then roll the cylinder over the sprinkles so they are embedded into the outside of the dough. Wrap up again and place in the fridge to chill for at least 30 minutes.
6. Cut the chilled cylinder of dough into 1cm slices with a sharp non-serrated knife.
7. Place on a lined baking sheet and bake at 180°c for 10-12 minutes, or until lightly golden round the edges.
8. Cool the cookies on the sheet before moving to a wire rack.

Perfect Chocolate Celebration Cake

Free-From:

Prep time: 15 minutes | Cooking time: 40-50 minutes | Makes 2 x 20cm cakes

One of my biggest early challenges when baking without milk, eggs and nuts was to create a perfect birthday cake. Cake is such a big feature of any child's birthday party and I always felt so sad that my daughters might not be able to experience the sheer joy of a spectacular themed cake. Over the years, this recipe has evolved and become my fool-proof, go-to celebration cake. The crumb is moist but not crumbly and is the perfect vehicle for a buttercream filling and/or fondant icing, ready for whatever decorations you would like. I hope this cake makes birthdays extra special for you too.

330g self-raising flour
45g or 5 tbsp cocoa powder
1½ tsp bicarbonate of soda
Pinch of salt
220g caster sugar
290ml dairy-free milk
100g dairy-free margarine, melted
2 tbsp dairy-free yoghurt
1 tsp vanilla extract

1. Preheat the oven to 180°c. Grease and line the base of two 20cm cake tins.
2. Sift the flour, cocoa, bicarbonate, and salt together, then stir in the sugar.
3. In a separate bowl, combine the milk, melted dairy-free margarine, yoghurt, and vanilla.
4. Make a well in the centre of the dry ingredients, pour in the wet ingredients and gradually combine until you have a lovely smooth batter.
5. Pour into the cake tins and bake for 25-30 minutes, until a knife comes out clean.
6. Cool in the tins for a few minutes, then turn out onto a wire rack.

Vanilla Buttercream

This makes more than enough for the cake above if filling and then doing a light coat to stick on the fondant. If you'd like to fill and generously coat the cake with buttercream, double the quantities.

145g dairy-free butter
250g icing sugar, sifted
1-2 tbsp dairy-free milk
1 tsp vanilla extract

1. Whisk the dairy-free butter until light and fluffy.
2. Add the icing sugar 100g at a time with a splash of the milk and vanilla, mixing until fully combined and fluffy.
3. If you want to use fondant icing for the decorations, use 500g to cover the cake and any offcuts for the decorations. Do be careful with the brand you buy as they often may contain traces of almonds.

Variations: Turn this into a chocolate fudge cake by replacing 25g of the icing sugar in the buttercream with cocoa powder.

Iced Buns

Free-From:

Prep time: 10 minutes, plus 1 hour 30 minutes proving | Baking time: 15 minutes | Makes 6

Taking centre stage in the window of any traditional English bakery, iced buns are perfect for a comforting treat on a cool autumn day. With their soft, sweet dough smothered in sugary sticky-sweet water icing, it's no surprise they're a perennial favourite. A fresh batch of these, adorned to your own tastes, gives any bakery a run for their money.

50g dairy-free margarine
150ml dairy-free milk
260g strong bread flour
50g caster sugar
1 tsp dried yeast
½ tsp salt

For the icing
175g icing sugar
1-2 tbsp water

1. Melt the margarine into the milk without making the temperature more than tepid.
2. Place the flour, sugar, yeast, and salt in a bowl, then pour in the warmed milk and margarine mixture. Bring to a dough and knead until smooth; it should bounce back when you press a finger onto the surface.
3. Place the dough in an oiled bowl, cover and leave to double in size in a warm place.
4. Divide into 6 even pieces and form into balls, then roll out into sausage shapes, trying to make them nice and even.
5. Place about 1cm apart on a lined baking sheet, cover and leave to rise for 30 minutes.
6. Preheat the oven to 190°c or 180°c fan and bake the buns for 15 minutes until golden, risen and sounding hollow when tapped on the base. Cool on a wire rack.
7. Meanwhile, mix the icing sugar and water together to form a very thick, smooth icing. Start by adding 1 tablespoon of water and gradually add more as required.
8. Once the buns are cool, top them with the thick water icing.

Variations: Why not make the icing pastel pink and add sprinkles? You could also split the buns in half horizontally and fill them with jam and dairy-free whipped cream for a luxurious alternative.

Caramel Crispy Bars

Free-From:

Prep time: 10 minutes | Chilling time: 1 hour | Makes about 16

Rice crispy cakes must be one of the first bakes than anyone makes, and they don't really deserve a place in a cookbook. But these caramel crispy bars are so much better than the usual chocolatey crispy cakes. Here, the caramel flavoured, gooey, crispy base is contrasted with a rich dark chocolate layer for the perfect balance of bitter and sweet. I have never known anyone to say no to one of these little squares, so if you want something quick, with minimal steps for crowd-pleasing results, this is the recipe for you.

120g caster sugar
170g golden syrup
100g Lotus Biscoff spread
100g Rice Krispies
120g dairy-free dark chocolate
10g dairy-free butter

1. Melt the sugar and syrup together until the sugar has dissolved. Stir in the Lotus Biscoff spread to make a thick, smooth mixture.
2. Stir in the Rice Krispies and ensure they are well covered with the syrupy mix.
3. Press into a lined baking tin (a 20cm square brownie tin is ideal) and place in the fridge to firm up for about 30 minutes.
4. Melt the dairy-free chocolate and butter together. Pour over the caramel crispy base and spread out. I like to make a pattern with a fork to make it look pretty.
5. Leave to set for another 30 minutes or so and then slice into squares or rectangles.

Variations: Don't fancy the chocolate? These bars are just as delicious with no topping, or you could add a handful of crushed pretzels before leaving them to set for a salty crunch.

Sticky Toffee Pudding

Free-From:

Prep time: 30 minutes | Baking time: 30-40 minutes | Makes 4 individual puddings

Sticky toffee pudding has almost mythical status in the pudding world, so I had to include my version in this book. To my mind, it is the essence of Autumn in pudding form. The sweetly spiced sponge laced with sticky dates (although you'd never know they were there, as they're blended to a pulp) and topped with warm toffee sauce makes the perfect cosy and comforting pudding.

100g dates, stoned and chopped
200ml dairy-free milk
½ tsp bicarbonate of soda
100g dairy-free margarine
60g soft brown sugar
1 tsp vanilla extract
125g self-raising flour
½ tsp ground ginger
¼ tsp ground cinnamon

For the sauce

50g golden syrup
60g soft brown sugar
175g dairy-free margarine or butter
½ tsp vanilla extract
50g dairy-free cream

1. Preheat the oven to 180°c and thoroughly grease 4 mini pudding moulds.
2. Add the dates to the dairy-free milk in a saucepan and simmer for 5-10 minutes, until the dates are soft. Using an immersion blender or food processor, blitz until smooth, then stir in the bicarbonate of soda and set aside to cool.
3. Cream the margarine and sugar together until light and fluffy. Stir in the vanilla. Pour in the date and milk mixture, stirring to combine everything.
4. Sift in the flour and spices. Gently mix to make a wet dough with no lumps of raw flour.
5. Half fill the pudding moulds and bake for 18-20 minutes until the sponge is set and golden.
6. Cool on a wire rack before removing the mould.
7. To make the sauce while the puddings are baking, melt the syrup, sugar, margarine, and vanilla together. Bring to the boil and simmer for 5 minutes. The sauce should thicken slightly. Remove from the heat and stir in the dairy-free cream.
8. Leave to cool a little, then pour the sauce over the sponges to serve.

Variations: To make a darker and stickier pudding, use soft dark brown sugar in the sponge, and for the sauce use just 30g of golden syrup along with 20g of molasses.

The Best Ever Chocolate Cookies

Free-From:

Prep time: 15 minutes, plus 1 hour chilling | Baking time: 11-12 minutes | Makes about 12-15

There is nothing like a chocolate cookie, but so often they're more average than amazing. These, however, are in the realms of awesome. They're the kind where you take a bite and immediately sigh with pleasure: deeply chocolatey, just the right kind of chew yet also crisp enough... these are up there with the very best.

75g dairy-free margarine
60g soft brown sugar
25g caster sugar
½ tsp good quality flaky salt, such as Maldon or fleur de sel
85g plain flour
15g good quality cocoa powder
Pinch of bicarbonate of soda
100g dairy-free chocolate, chopped

1. Cream the margarine, sugars, and salt together.
2. Gently mix in the flour, cocoa and bicarbonate to form a soft dough.
3. Stir in the chopped chocolate until evenly distributed.
4. Form the dough into a sausage shape and wrap in baking parchment or cling film. Place in the fridge to chill: you want it to be as cold as possible. If preferred, you can freeze the dough at this point and then bake from frozen, adding an extra 2 minutes to the baking time.
5. Preheat the oven to 170°c and line two baking sheets with parchment.
6. Cut the chilled or frozen cookie dough into 1cm slices and place well apart on the baking sheets. Bake for 11-12 minutes. They should spread out nicely.
7. Cool briefly on the sheets so they are stiff enough to move and then transfer to a wire rack.

Marvellous Muffins

Muffins are just marvellous, lighter than a cupcake and so flavoursome they don't need any icing or dressing up. I have gone for traditional blueberry because you can't go wrong with such a classic, and a seasonal sweetly spiced option. Who needs a latte when you can have a pumpkin spice muffin instead?

Pumpkin Spice Muffins

Free-From:

Prep time: 15 minutes | Baking time: 18-20 minutes | Makes 6 large muffins

150g plain flour
25g soft brown sugar
20g caster sugar
½ tbsp baking powder
Pinch of salt
80ml each dairy-free milk and yoghurt
55g dairy-free margarine, melted
20ml golden or maple syrup
Sugar crystals, for decoration (optional)

For the pumpkin spice

50g caster sugar
1 tsp each ground ginger and cinnamon
Pinch of ground nutmeg
¼ tsp mixed spice

1. Preheat the oven to 180°c and fill a muffin tray with paper cases.
2. To make the pumpkin spice, simply mix all the ingredients together and store in a sealed jar. It's also great in homemade lattes, hot chocolates, cookies and cakes.
3. Mix all the dry ingredients for the muffins together along with 3 teaspoons of your pumpkin spice. Pour in the wet ingredients and combine. You do not want any clumps of raw flour but do not overmix the batter, a little lumpy is good.
4. Quarter fill the paper cases and then sprinkle half a teaspoon of pumpkin spice over each one. Cover with the remaining muffin mix.
5. Top each of the muffins with another half teaspoon of the pumpkin spice, plus a sprinkle of sugar crystals (if using).
6. Bake for 18-20 minutes, or until risen and golden and a knife comes out clean. Remove from the oven and leave the muffins to cool on a wire rack.

Blueberry Muffins

Free-From:

Prep time: 15 minutes | Baking time: 18-20 minutes | Makes 6 large muffins

165g plain flour
85g caster sugar
½ tbsp cornflour
½ tsp baking powder
¼ tsp bicarbonate of soda
Pinch of salt
½ lemon, zested (optional)
100ml dairy-free milk
35g dairy-free margarine, melted
½ tbsp lemon juice
50g blueberries

1. Preheat the oven to 190°c and line a muffin tray with paper cases.
2. Mix the dry ingredients together and add the lemon zest if using.
3. Combine the milk, melted margarine and lemon juice. Pour into the dry ingredients.
4. Gently mix so the batter is a bit lumpy but there are no patches of raw flour, then stir in the blueberries.
5. Two thirds fill each paper case and bake for 18-20 minutes until well risen and golden.
6. Take out the tin and leave the muffins to cool on a wire rack.

Light and Airy Chocolate Mousse with 'Pain au Chocolat' Palmiers

I hope this mousse really impresses you. The texture is so light and airy you'd be forgiven for thinking you were eating a chocolate cloud. While the mousse is wonderful alone or with a side of fresh berries, the addition of sweet and crunchy chocolate palmiers adds texture. The palmiers also make a great snack on their own and are a wonderful way of using up leftover puff pastry.

Chocolate Mousse

Free-From:

Prep time: 20 minutes | Chilling time: minimum 1 hour | Serves 4

80ml aquafaba (the water from a tin of beans or chickpeas, make sure there is no added salt)
1/8 tsp cream of tartar
2 tbsp caster sugar
100g dairy-free dark chocolate
125ml dairy-free double or whipping cream
1 tsp vanilla paste

1. Using a stand mixer or a handheld electric whisk, beat the aquafaba with the cream of tartar until it forms light clouds of meringue-style foam. Beat in the sugar a tablespoon at a time until you have firm peaks. Set aside.
2. Melt the chocolate either over a bain-marie or in a microwave, then stir in the dairy-free cream a little at a time so the mixture doesn't seize up. Stir in the vanilla paste.
3. Beat a quarter of the meringue mix into the chocolate cream to slacken the mixture. Gently fold in the rest of the meringue mixture, trying to keep as much volume as possible.
4. Pour the mousse mixture into 4 ramekins, level off the tops and place in the fridge for at least an hour to set.

Variations: How about a minty After Eight mousse? Add a drop or two of peppermint essence instead of the vanilla and garnish with a mint leaf. Be cautious with the peppermint essence as it's extremely strong, so add one drop at a time and taste, taste, taste.

'Pain au Chocolat' Palmiers

Free-From:

Prep time: 10 minutes | Baking time: 15-20 minutes | Makes about 20

1 tbsp dairy-free margarine
1 tbsp cocoa powder
½ pack of ready-made puff pastry
45g caster sugar, plus 3-4 tbsp for rolling

1. Preheat the oven to 200°c and line a baking sheet with parchment paper.
2. Combine the margarine and cocoa powder, then set aside.
3. Roll out the pastry, using caster sugar rather than flour to prevent it from sticking, until it forms a nice large rectangle.
4. Spread the cocoa mix evenly over the pastry and then sprinkle with a fine layer of caster sugar.
5. Fold the pastry like a book, bringing the short sides up to meet in the middle. Repeat this folding twice more, so you have made 3 folds in total.
6. Cut the folded pastry into 1cm slices and place well apart on the baking sheet.
7. Bake the palmiers for 15-20 minutes, or until golden and crisp.

Salted, Poppy Seed or Cinnamon Sugar Pretzel Knots

Free-From:

Prep time: 2 hours (including proving) | Baking time: 12-15 minutes | Makes 12

The beauty of these pretzels is not just that they're cute and delicious, but you can make one batch of dough and end up with savoury rolls – which are great for sandwiches or even burgers – as well as sweet doughnut-like treats. Now that makes it more than worthwhile! I like to make all three varieties from one batch of dough, but you can just as easily stick to one of the flavours instead.

500g strong bread flour
1 tsp salt
1 tbsp fast-action dried yeast
2 tbsp maple syrup or golden syrup
1 tbsp oil
250-300ml water
2 tbsp bicarbonate of soda

Either
1 tbsp salt
2 tbsp poppy seeds

Or
2 tsp cinnamon
3 tbsp caster sugar
2 tbsp dairy-free margarine, melted

1. Put the flour and salt into a bowl, add the yeast, then pour in the syrup, oil and water. Bring together to form a soft but not sticky dough and then knead until silky smooth and bouncy. This will take up to 10 minutes.
2. Cover and leave to prove. The dough should double in size, which will take an hour or so.
3. Divide the dough into 12 even pieces and roll them into loose balls. Cover and leave to rest for 10 minutes. Meanwhile, preheat the oven to 220°c or 200°c fan.
4. Roll each ball into a 30cm long sausage shape with tapering ends. Form this into a U shape, bring the ends together, twist twice and then attach to the U to give a pretzel knot. Keep the finished knots covered with a tea towel.
5. Bring a saucepan of water to the boil, stir in the bicarbonate of soda and then add the pretzel knots in batches of 3, cooking them for 15 seconds on each side. Remove from the pan with a slotted spoon and place on a baking sheet.
6. For savoury pretzels, sprinkle with the salt and/or poppy seeds while they are still damp. For sweet pretzels, leave ungarnished.
7. Bake for 12-15 minutes until they have risen and have a lovely burnished bronzed appearance. Remove from the oven and cool on a wire rack.
8. For sweet pretzels, combine the cinnamon and sugar in a large shallow bowl. Brush each cooled pretzel with the melted margarine and then roll in the cinnamon sugar until they are completely coated. Eat as soon as possible.

Top Tip: Make a honey and mustard dip for savoury pretzels. Simply mix together equal quantities of Dijon mustard and honey or maple syrup to taste.

Autumn Berry Crumble Bars

Free-From:

Prep time: 20 minutes | Baking time: 45-50 minutes | Makes 6 bars in a 2lb loaf tin, easily doubled for 12 bars in a square tin

These gorgeously fruity, oaty, seeded crumble bars are inspired by a Yotam Ottolenghi recipe, so they have great heritage on the flavour front. I see them as a mixture of jam tarts, berry crumble, a hint of flapjack, and a smidgen of cereal bar, and it's a rather delightful combination.

60g plain flour
35g oats
30g caster sugar
¼ tsp baking powder
Pinch of salt
50g dairy-free butter, fridge cold
6 tbsp your favourite jam (about half a jar)

For the crumble top

30g plain flour
20g oats
12g demerara sugar
15g dairy-free butter, fridge cold

For the candied seeds

15g caster sugar
15g dairy-free butter
10ml dairy free milk
15g oats
15g pumpkin seeds
15g sunflower seeds

1. Preheat the oven to 170°c and line a loaf tin with non-stick baking paper.
2. Pour the flour, caster sugar, oats, baking powder, and salt into a bowl. Cut the butter into small cubes and rub into the dry mix with your fingertips until it resembles fine breadcrumbs.
3. Lightly press the mix into the base of the lined tin and bake for 20 minutes until lightly golden around the edges. Remove from the oven and leave to cool.
4. While the base is cooking, make the crumble top. Place the flour, oats and demerara sugar into a bowl. Cut the butter into small cubes and rub in until you have a craggy crumble.
5. To make the candied seeds, melt the sugar, butter and milk together until the sugar has dissolved. Stir in the oats and seeds.
6. Once the base has cooled a little, spread over the jam in an even layer. Spread the seeds over the jam, then sprinkle over the crumble topping.
7. Bake for 25-30 minutes, until the top is golden brown.
8. Let it cool fully in the tin before cutting into slices. These bars keep for a good week in an airtight container.

Mini Devil's Food Cakes

Free-From:

Prep time: 20 minutes | Baking time: 20 minutes | Makes 12

I nearly didn't include this recipe as there are other chocolate cakes in this book, but in the end, I knew it deserved to have a place. The sponge is so rich and moist, and the fudgy icing is maybe the most delicious chocolatey mixture you could imagine. I just couldn't leave them out! These have equal standing as a pudding or a cake, but no matter how you serve them, they'll go down a storm.

120ml hot water
25g cocoa powder
120ml dairy-free milk
80g golden syrup or maple syrup
60ml sunflower oil
1 tsp white wine vinegar
1 tsp vanilla extract
55g caster sugar
135g plain flour
1 tsp baking powder
1 tsp bicarbonate of soda
Pinch of salt

For the icing
100g dairy-free dark chocolate
60g dairy-free margarine
50g icing sugar
1 tbsp dairy-free milk
½ tbsp golden syrup or maple syrup

1. Preheat the oven to 180°c. Line 12 silicone cake moulds of your choice. I like to use dome or ring shapes but a usual cupcake tray with paper cases will be fine too.
2. Whisk together the hot water and cocoa. Mix in the milk, golden syrup, oil, vinegar, and vanilla. Next, stir in the sugar until it has dissolved.
3. Sift in the flour, baking powder, bicarbonate of soda, and salt. Mix to form a very wet cake batter, making sure there are no lumps of flour left.
4. Pour or pipe the batter into the mini cake cases or silicone moulds and bake for 15-20 minutes, or until a knife comes out clean.
5. Cool in the tin before removing and transferring to a wire rack. If you've used a silicone mould, freeze the cakes for half an hour before attempting to remove from the mould.
6. Meanwhile, melt the icing ingredients together and simmer for 2 minutes until thick and glossy. Let it cool slightly before using.
7. Pour the icing over the cooled cakes so they have a nice thick topping. Decorate if desired and leave to set before serving.

WINTER

Winter may be the darkest time of year but it's also one of the most exciting, with the prospect of joyful twinkly lights and decorations, Christmas and new year festivities, and cosying up in front of roaring open fires. There are many festive bakes you can't easily buy for those who want or need to avoid certain ingredients, so here you'll find my friendly versions of Christmas cakes, snacks, chocolates, sweets and showstopping puddings, all of which need not be only for Christmas of course.

Churros Cake with Warm Chocolate Ganache Sauce

Drawing inspiration from the famous Spanish doughnut-like treat, here we have a lightly fluffy sponge, rippled with a spicy sweet cinnamon swirl, sprinkled with a crunchy sugar coating: just like churros in cake form. It really is as delicious as it sounds! Add a warm, dark chocolate ganache sauce (which also makes a delicious ice cream topping) and you're in churros cake heaven.

Churros Cake

Free-From:

Prep time: 15 minutes | Baking time: 30-35 minutes | Makes 1 Bundt cake or a 2lb/1kg loaf cake

370g self-raising flour
2 tbsp custard powder or cornflour
1½ tsp bicarbonate of soda
1 tsp ground cinnamon
Pinch of salt
220g caster sugar
290ml dairy-free milk
2 tbsp dairy-free yoghurt
100g dairy-free margarine, melted
40g soft brown sugar mixed with 1 tsp ground cinnamon
2 tbsp caster sugar

1. Preheat the oven to 180°c. If using a Bundt tin, generously grease it with margarine.
2. Sift the flour, custard powder, bicarbonate of soda, cinnamon and salt into a large bowl.
3. Stir the caster sugar into the dry ingredients. In a separate bowl, mix the dairy-free milk, yoghurt and melted margarine together.
4. Stir the wet ingredients into the dry until well combined.
5. Pour one third of the batter into the cake tin, sprinkle over half the cinnamon sugar and then repeat, finishing with the last third of the batter. Gently marble the batter with a skewer and bake for 30-35 minutes, until a knife comes out clean.
6. If using a Bundt tin, leave the cake in the tin until fully cool.
7. Sprinkle with the extra caster sugar before serving.

Warm Chocolate Ganache Sauce

Free-From:

Prep time: 5 minutes | Serves 2

50g dark chocolate
3 tbsp dairy-free cream

1. Melt the chocolate and cream together until smooth and fully combined.
2. Serve warm.

Savoury Nibbles

Everyone loves a savoury snack, but the options can be limited if you have to avoid certain very common ingredients. In these recipes I've recreated those unfailingly popular British classics, Mini Cheddars and 'love them or hate them' Marmite flavoured Twiglets. My cheddar-free mini biscuits are not quite as cheesy as the real thing but have a lovely tangy note and they do a great job of replicating the original. The homemade Twiglets are a party for your tastebuds: savoury, umami, crunchy... what's not to like!

Mini 'Cheesy' Biscuits

Free-From:

Prep time: 10-15 minutes | Baking time: 10-12 minutes | Makes 30-35

140g plain flour
3 tbsp nutritional yeast
1 tsp English mustard powder
¼ - ½ tsp salt
Large pinch of cayenne pepper
75g dairy-free butter
1-2 tbsp cold water

1. Preheat the oven to 180°c. In a food processor, pulse together the flour, yeast, mustard powder, salt, cayenne, and butter. Or, rub the fat into the flour mix with your fingertips.
2. Add 1 tablespoon of the cold water and continue to pulse or mix until you have formed a soft but not sticky dough. Add more cold water if required and if the dough is sticky, add a touch more flour.
3. Roll out the dough to 3mm thick, stamp out small circles (about 3cm diameter) and place them onto a baking sheet. Repeat to use up all the dough.
4. Prick the centres with a fork to create the correct Mini Cheddar look, then bake for 10-12 minutes until starting to turn golden brown. Cool on a wire rack.

My Take on Twiglets

Free-From:

Prep time: 30 minutes | Baking time: 15-20 minutes | Makes about 80

½ tsp salt
125g wholemeal flour
2 tsp yeast extract
40ml extra virgin olive oil
40ml water
1 tsp yeast extract mixed with 1 tsp dairy-free milk, to glaze
Flaky salt crystals

1. Stir the salt into the flour. Add the yeast extract, olive oil and water. Bring everything together to form a soft dough, then knead until silky and smooth.
2. Wrap and rest the dough in the fridge for at least an hour. Preheat the oven to 190°c or 180°c fan.
3. Take small grape sized pieces of the chilled dough and then roll into 0.5cm thick sausages. Cut the sausages into bite-size stick lengths and try to make them uneven and gnarly.
4. Place the sticks on a lined baking tray while you shape the rest and bring a pan of water to the boil. Drop in the sticks, ten or so at a time, and boil until they rise to the surface. This will take around 30 seconds. Place them back on the lined baking sheet.
5. Brush the sticks with the glaze and sprinkle with the flaky salt, then bake for 15-20 minutes until golden brown and crispy.
6. Cool on a wire rack. These will get crunchier as they cool. Store in an airtight container for up to a week, if they last that long!

Gingerbread

Free-From:

Prep time: 15 minutes | Baking time: 10-12 minutes | Makes 12-15 cookies

We love this recipe so much that we end up having gingerbread all year round, not just at Christmas. The addition of cream cheese makes the resulting biscuits either meltingly soft like a freshly baked cookie or crunchy like the gingerbread biscuits you buy, depending on how long you bake them for. Whichever way you prefer them, they are delicious. Gingerbread is lovely unadorned, but we like to decorate them with fondant or water icing for a more festive feel.

50g dairy-free margarine
20g dairy-free cream cheese
75g soft brown sugar
2 tbsp golden syrup
20ml dairy-free milk
170g plain flour
1 tsp ground ginger
½ tsp bicarbonate of soda
1 tbsp icing sugar
250g roll out fondant icing

1. Cream the margarine, cream cheese, sugar, syrup, and milk together.
2. Sift in the flour, ground ginger and bicarbonate of soda. Knead into a soft dough.
3. On a floured surface, roll out the dough to 0.5cm thickness. Cut into shapes with shaped cookie cutters and place on a greased baking sheet.
4. Bake the gingerbread for 10-12 minutes at 190°c (10 minutes for soft, 12 for crisp).
5. Cool on the sheet a little before transferring to a wire rack.
6. Make a little icing 'glue' by mixing the icing sugar with 1 teaspoon of water.
7. Roll out the fondant icing, dusting the surface with icing sugar, and cut out shapes with the same cookie cutter you used for the gingerbread.
8. Spread a little icing 'glue' on each cookie to attach the fondant icing shapes. Alternatively, pipe decorations onto the gingerbread with a thick water icing.

Variations: Why not make tiny bite-size star shaped cookies? Press some crunchy sugar into the top and then bake for 8 minutes.

To Father
Christmas
and Rudolph

Christmas Chocolates

Sadly, there is still a lack of interesting and inclusive chocolates, which is especially noticeable at Christmas time when everyone else is tucking into tempting selection boxes. But fear not, it's very simple to make your own delightful after dinner treats that anyone can have. These homemade crisp chocolate sticks with crunchy flavoured sugar crystals are just like Matchmakers and my cool peppermint creams are just as delicious as the originals. Use free-from chocolate and these are suitable for most to enjoy.

My Homemade Matchmakers

Free-From:

Prep time: 5 minutes (20 if tempering) | Makes 12-14

2 tbsp demerara sugar or coarse granulated sugar
½ - 1 tsp orange essence or ½ tsp mint essence
85g dairy-free dark chocolate

1. Add the essence of your choice to the sugar, stir well and then leave to dry out for 10 or so minutes. I'd advise tasting the sugar once the essence is added, as you may want to add more essence depending on how much flavour you like in your chocolate sticks.
2. Meanwhile, line a baking sheet with baking parchment and place in the fridge.
3. Ideally, temper the chocolate (see instructions on page 18) or just gently melt until it is completely fluid.
4. Stir the flavoured sugar into the chocolate. Transfer to a piping bag and snip off the tip; you want an opening of about 4mm.
5. Pipe long straight lines of chocolate onto the chilled baking sheet. Leave to set. If the chocolate is not tempered, you will need to keep these in the fridge.

Peppermint Creams

Free-From:

Prep time: 12 hours (including drying time) | Makes 22-24

320g icing sugar, sifted
40g dairy-free margarine, melted
½ tsp peppermint essence
1 tbsp water
130g dairy-free dark chocolate

1. Place the sifted icing sugar in a large bowl, then pour in the melted margarine, peppermint essence and water.
2. Mix to form a soft (but not sticky) dough. If it's too wet, add more icing sugar and if dry, add more water.
3. Knead lightly on a surface dusted with icing sugar to make the dough smooth. Roll out, using icing sugar rather than flour, to 0.5cm thickness and cut out disc shapes with a cookie cutter.
4. Place the shapes on a lined baking sheet and leave in a cool place overnight to dry out. Make sure you turn them so they dry on both sides.
5. Melt the chocolate in a microwave or over a bain-marie until the chocolate is fully fluid. Ideally follow the tempering guidelines on page 18. Once the chocolate is tempered, dip in the creams so they are fully submerged and completely coated.
6. Place back on the lined baking sheet and leave to set, then keep in a cool place or the fridge.

Top Tip: To make it easier to coat the peppermint creams, add 10g of cocoa butter (melted to 45°c) to the liquified or tempered chocolate.

Cinnamon Buns

Free-From:

Prep time: 30 minutes, plus 1 hour 30 minutes proving | Baking time: 17-20 minutes | Makes about 6 (easily doubled or quadrupled!)

When the girls were younger, I used to bake something for them to take into school every Friday to share with their classmates, because I wanted them to have the opportunity to enjoy treats with their friends, as they couldn't have most of the goodies the teachers or other parents made or bought. I hope it also educated other young people that 'friendly' food can be just as good, or even better. It certainly helped hone my baking skills, and these cinnamon buns were some of the most frequently requested bakes for Friday cake day.

250g strong bread flour
25g caster sugar
1 tbsp cornflour
1½ tsp dried yeast
½ tsp cinnamon
Pinch of salt
150ml dairy-free milk, at room temperature
30g dairy-free margarine, softened

For the filling

2 tsp cinnamon
25g soft brown sugar
1 tbsp dairy-free margarine

For the glaze

1 tbsp soft brown sugar
1 tbsp water
1 tbsp pearl sugar or sugar crystals (optional)
50g icing sugar (optional)

1. In a bowl, mix the flour, sugar, cornflour, yeast, cinnamon, and salt. Make a well in the centre and pour in the tepid milk, then add the soft margarine.
2. Bring everything together to form a soft dough and knead until smooth and bouncing back. This will take 5-10 minutes.
3. Cover and let the dough double in size which will take an hour or more.
4. Meanwhile, combine the cinnamon, sugar and margarine in a small bowl to make a paste.
5. Knock back and roll out the dough to a 24 by 30cm rectangle. Spread the cinnamon sugar paste over the whole of the dough rectangle and then roll up to form a tight cylinder.
6. Cut the cylinder into 4cm slices and place them on a lined baking sheet. Press down slightly, loosely cover and then leave to rise again for 30 minutes.
7. Preheat the oven to 180°c. Bake the buns for 17-20 minutes until risen, golden and cooked through.
8. Meanwhile, melt the brown sugar into the water in a small saucepan. Bring to the boil and then turn off the heat. Brush the glaze over the top of the warm buns and then sprinkle with the pearl sugar (if using).
9. Remove the buns from the pans and let them cool completely on a wire rack.
10. If you like, combine the icing sugar with enough water to make a runny icing, then drizzle this over the buns before serving.

Crème Brûlée with Shortbread Bites

Crème brûlée is an unfailingly popular dessert, so I had to make my own friendly version. A rich, unctuous, vanilla-scented cream topped with a wonderfully crisp glaze to crack… pudding perfection! Why not serve it with some shortbread bites for a lovely textural contrast?

Crème Brûlée

Free-From:

Prep time: 20 minutes | Chilling time: 1 hour | Serves 4

1½ tbsp cornflour
1½ tbsp dairy-free milk
250ml dairy-free double cream
45g caster sugar
1 tsp vanilla extract, or the seeds scraped from ½ a vanilla pod
2 tbsp granulated sugar

1. Mix the cornflour and milk together to form a smooth liquid, then set aside.
2. Heat the cream with the sugar until the sugar has dissolved, then stir in the vanilla.
3. Next, stir in the cornflour mix and increase the heat. Whisk until the cream has thickened to thick yoghurt consistency. This should happen once the mixture comes to a boil.
4. Pour the creamy mixture into 4 ramekins and place in the fridge to firm up.
5. Once set, sprinkle an even layer of sugar over the top.
6. Caramelise with a blow torch or under the grill. Eat within an hour to make sure the caramel remains crispy. If eating the next day, prepare the set custard and then add the sugar and grill or blowtorch it just before serving.

Variations: Why not add a small handful of raspberries to the ramekins under the custard, or perhaps add lemon zest instead of the vanilla. Another nice variation is using espresso coffee rather than the milk to slake the cornflour, to make a rather delightful coffee crème brûlée.

Shortbread Bites

Free-From:

Prep time: 30 minutes (including resting time) | Baking time: 10-12 minutes | Makes about 20

75g soft brown sugar
1 tsp vanilla extract
¼ tsp salt
225g plain flour
150g dairy-free butter
1 tbsp crunchy sugar, such as demerara or granulated (optional)

1. Heat the oven to 160°c and line a baking sheet with parchment paper.
2. Stir the sugar, vanilla, and salt into the flour. Rub in the butter with your fingertips (you need a light touch with shortbread) and then squeeze gently to form a crumbly dough.
3. Roll out the dough between two sheets of parchment paper and then sprinkle with the crunchy sugar. Roll out a little more until it is 0.5cm thick and then chill in the fridge for 20 minutes.
4. Stamp out or cut out small shapes from the chilled dough. Place on the lined baking sheet and bake for 10-12 minutes, then leave to cool on a wire rack.

Variations: Why not use the zest of a lemon instead of the vanilla or add half a teaspoon of ground cinnamon for some mellow spice.

Tiffin Wreath Cake

Free-From:

Prep time: 15 minutes | Chilling time: 1 hour minimum | Serves 8-12

Here's one for people who don't want to make a fruitcake but still want an eye-catching Christmas centrepiece. The beauty of this recipe is that it's incredibly easy to make but looks spectacular and worthy of the Christmas table, even more so in a ring-shaped cake tin or Bundt tin. You can just make a plain tiffin in a square cake tin, and everyone will still love it, but making a wreath shape and topping it with some white chocolate snow makes this a proper festive showpiece. Use allergen-free chocolate and gluten-free biscuits to make this a showstopper for more to enjoy.

170g dairy-free chocolate
120g dairy-free butter or margarine
3 tbsp golden or maple syrup
12 biscuits, roughly crushed
20g crispy rice cereal
50g white chocolate
Christmas decorations

1. Line a Bundt tin or cake tin with 2 layers of cling film.
2. Melt the chocolate, margarine, and syrup together. Stir well to form a gorgeous truffle mixture, then fold in the crushed biscuits and rice cereal.
3. Pour the tiffin mixture into the lined tin and bring the cling film over the top so it is entirely covered. Press down firmly for a compacted centre and even top.
4. Place in the fridge for at least a couple of hours to firm up.
5. Melt the white chocolate and drizzle it over the top, then add your decorations and leave to set before serving.

Christmas Cake

Free-From:

Prep time: overnight, plus 20 minutes | Baking time: 45-55 minutes | Makes 1 x 22-24cm cake

This is a brilliant Christmas cake recipe, although there's no reason why you couldn't enjoy it at any time of year as a teatime treat. It's rich with plenty of dried fruit but remains light and moist. It's so good it's even been finished in just two sittings, which is quite an achievement for a large fruit cake!

2 tbsp brandy or apple juice
50g mixed peel, chopped
100g dates, stoned and chopped
200g sultanas
200g currants
350g plain flour
½ tsp cinnamon
½ tsp mixed spice
¼ tsp salt
1 lemon, zested
70g dairy-free butter
170g light Muscovado sugar
1 tsp bicarbonate of soda
250ml dairy-free milk, warmed to hand hot temperature

To soak and decorate (optional)

Extra brandy or apple juice
3 tbsp apricot jam, melted
500g fondant icing, rolled out

1. Pour the brandy or apple juice over the dried fruit and leave to steep for at least a couple of hours, or preferably overnight.
2. Preheat the oven to 180°c. Grease and line a 22 or 24cm cake tin.
3. Sift the flour, cinnamon, mixed spice, and salt into a large bowl. Add the lemon zest.
4. Rub the dairy-free butter into the flour mixture until it resembles fine breadcrumbs. Stir in the sugar and the steeped dried fruit.
5. Add the bicarbonate of soda to the warm milk and stir until dissolved. Pour this into the dry ingredients and mix to form a very stiff batter.
6. Turn into the lined cake tin, level off the top and bake for 35 minutes. Turn the oven down to 160°c and continue to bake for a further 10-20 minutes, or until a knife comes out clean, checking regularly to make sure it doesn't overbake.
7. Turn the cake out of the tin and leave to cool on a wire rack.
8. Once completely cool, keep the cake wrapped in baking paper in an airtight container until ready to decorate (if desired) just before Christmas.
9. For added moisture and flavour, pour 1 tablespoon of apple juice or brandy onto the cake each week until ready to use.
10. To cover the cake for decorating, brush it with the melted apricot jam and then cover with the fondant icing.

Pomegranate Fruit Jellies

Free-From:

Prep time: 40 minutes | Setting time: 2 hours | Makes 50-100 jellies

These fruity sweets are traditional French pâte de fruits: soft and yielding sugar-coated jellies that are often for sale at Christmas time. Made with natural, all vegetarian and allergen-free ingredients but packed full of intense fruity flavour, these jellies make a wonderful after dinner sweet or a gift for any occasion.

500ml pure pomegranate juice
1 lime, juiced
75g glucose syrup
15g pectin
450g granulated sugar
3 tbsp grenadine
1 tsp flavourless oil
50g caster sugar, for rolling

1. Line a 20cm square baking tin with parchment paper.
2. Pour the juices and syrup into a deep saucepan. Stir the pectin powder into half of the sugar, then sprinkle this over the juice and stir while heating gently until the sugar has dissolved.
3. Add the rest of the sugar to the pan along with the grenadine and oil. Let the sugar dissolve, then bring the mixture to a rolling boil.
4. The temperature needs to reach 110°c. This will take 10-15 minutes and you will notice the bubbles changing as the mixture heats. Be sure to scrape down the sides while the mixture is bubbling.
5. As soon as it reaches 110°c, take the pan off the heat and pour the mixture into the lined tin.
6. Leave to cool, then cover with baking parchment. Once fully cold and set, cut into pretty shapes. Squares or triangles are the most efficient, but I like using mini cookie cutters to stamp out little shapes.
7. Roll each jelly in caster sugar and then store in an airtight container until ready to eat.

Herb Fougasse with Green Olive Tapenade

I started making fougasse during the first Covid lockdown in 2020, when every Friday night I recreated food from some of our favourite restaurants to add some excitement to the endless weeks at home. I even designed and made the correct menus, decorations, and playlists to match which was lots of fun! My French bistro at home featured herby leaf-shaped fougasse loaves, which were such a hit that they've become a regular sharing starter, which we serve with green olive tapenade or a simple oil and balsamic dip.

Herb Fougasse

Free-From:

Prep time: 1 hour 30 minutes (including proving) | Baking time: 15-20 minutes | Makes 2 large leaf shapes, enough for 8 people

500g strong white bread flour, plus extra for dusting
1½ tsp fine table salt
1 tbsp instant yeast
2 tbsp olive oil, plus extra for drizzling
300-350ml warm water
1 tbsp chopped fresh rosemary
1 tsp chopped fresh thyme
1 tsp dried herbes de Provence
1 tbsp polenta mixed with 1 tbsp flour, for dusting
1 tsp dried oregano
Flaky sea salt

1. Line 2 large baking sheets with baking parchment.
2. Put the flour, fine table salt and yeast into a bowl, ideally using a stand mixer. Add the olive oil and 300ml of the water. If it looks dry once mixed, add more of the water.
3. Add the rosemary, thyme and herbes de Provence, then knead for 5-10 minutes until the dough is smooth and springy.
4. Cover and leave to rise until at least doubled in size. This will take at least an hour.
5. Heavily dust a work surface with the flour and polenta mix. Carefully tip out the dough and divide it equally in half.
6. Press out each piece into an oval shape and lift onto the prepared baking sheets. Using a pizza cutter, make 2 cuts down the centre line and then 5 smaller diagonal cuts on each side to form the leaf veins. These should go all the way through the dough. Stretch out the holes with your fingers.
7. Place the baking sheets inside large plastic bags, seal and leave to prove in a warm place for 20 minutes. Preheat the oven to 220°c or 200°c fan.
8. Brush the risen loaves with olive oil, sprinkle over the oregano and flaky salt, then bake for 15–20 minutes, or until the fougasse sounds hollow when tapped on the base.
9. Remove from the oven and eat while still warm.

Green Olive Tapenade

Free-From:

Prep time: 5 minutes | Makes 1 small bowlful

100g pitted green olives, rinsed
1 small clove of garlic, minced
1 tsp Dijon mustard (optional)
1 tsp wine vinegar
3 tbsp extra virgin olive oil
Squeeze of lemon juice
Salt, to taste

1. In a food processor, whizz together the olives, garlic, mustard, and vinegar until well chopped.
2. With the motor running, drizzle in the oil until you have the desired consistency (we like it smooth). For chunkier tapenade, use less oil.
3. Taste and add the lemon juice if needed, then season with salt.

Cheat's Profiteroles

Free-From:

Prep time: 30 minutes | Baking time: 15 minutes | Makes 12 large buns

This recipe forces puff pastry to behave a bit like a choux bun. Yes, I admit it's a cheat, but it's almost impossible to make a good egg-free choux, which is what I'm after here, and this does the job very well. Once you add the filling and sauce to the hollow puff pastry buns, you really do get a profiterole effect.

1 sheet of ready-rolled puff pastry

For the crème pâtissière

300ml dairy-free milk
50g caster sugar
1 tsp vanilla extract or the seeds from 1 vanilla pod
15g plain flour
15g cornflour

For the chocolate ganache sauce

50g dairy-free dark chocolate
50g dairy-free cream
1 tsp golden syrup

1. Preheat the oven to 240°c and line a muffin or cupcake tray with paper cases.
2. Use a glass with a thick rim (not a cookie cutter) to cut out circles of pastry. You need the glass to squash and fuse together the edges of the dough, making a seal so the middle can puff up to create an airy little container. If you were to use a cookie cutter, this would not happen as the layers would be sliced right through.
3. Place the pastry circles on the paper cases so they sit above the base. Gently push down in the middle a little but they must be mainly resting on the top.
4. Place in the preheated oven for 6-7 minutes until the circles have completely puffed up (keep a close eye on them as this is the crucial part).
5. Once they've puffed up, reduce the oven temperature to 150°c and cook for a further 6-8 minutes until golden brown. Remove from the tray and liners and cool on a wire rack.
6. To make the crème pâtissière, pour the milk, sugar and vanilla into a saucepan. Heat until it reaches simmering point.
7. In a bowl, stir 2 tablespoons of the hot milk mixture into the flour and cornflour to make a smooth paste. Pour this paste into the remaining milk mixture and stir well.
8. Whisk while bringing to the boil. The mixture should start to thicken. Keep whisking the boiling mix for a couple of minutes, then pour into a container and cover so that the cling film is touching the top to prevent a skin forming. Leave to cool.
9. To make the chocolate ganache, simply melt the ingredients together until smooth and luscious.
10. To assemble the profiteroles, whisk up the cooled crème pâtissière to make it smooth and then place into a piping bag with a plain nozzle. With the nozzle of the piping bag, make a small hole in each puff pastry bun and pipe in the pastry cream.
11. Drizzle the chocolate ganache sauce over the filled buns, then leave for at least 30 minutes so the buns can soften and gain a choux-like texture.

Mocha Biscotti with Extravagant Hot Chocolate

Uniquely crunchy, biscotti are a Tuscan classic that adds a different dimension to the usual biscuit world. Also known as cantucci, these twice-baked oblong biscuits are traditionally dipped into a drink, often Vin Santo. This version combines a light coffee flavour with chocolate for a mocha vibe and are superb when served with a mug of rich hot chocolate for dipping into. Perfect for a cold winter's night.

Mocha Biscotti

Free-From:

Prep time: 20 minutes | Baking time: 35-40 minutes | Makes about 24 biscotti

250g plain flour
2 tsp baking powder
Pinch of salt
200g caster sugar
50g dairy-free chocolate, chopped
1 tbsp instant coffee powder
1 tbsp hot water
100ml dairy-free milk (approximately)
120ml sunflower oil
30g dairy-free chocolate, melted

1. Preheat the oven to 180°c and line two cookie sheets with baking parchment.
2. Sift the flour, baking powder and salt into a large bowl. Stir in the sugar and chopped chocolate.
3. Mix the instant coffee with the hot water in a jug, then top up to 120ml with the dairy-free milk.
4. Make a well in the centre of the flour mix and pour in the coffee-flavoured milk and the oil. Bring together to make a wet and sticky dough.
5. Form the dough into 1 or 2 log shapes on the lined baking sheet. They do spread out quite a lot so make them smaller than you think, unless you want long biscotti! Brush the logs with a little dairy-free milk.
6. Bake for 25-30 minutes until cooked through and starting to turn golden around the edges.
7. Cool briefly, then cut into even slices. Return the slices to the baking sheet and bake for a further 5 minutes, turn the slices over and cook for 5 more minutes. You want a uniform slightly golden tinge, but no particularly dark areas.
8. Cool the biscotti on a wire rack. Once completely cool, drizzle or dip into the melted chocolate. These keep well, in an airtight container for a week or so.

Extravagant Hot Chocolate

Free-From:

Prep time: 5 minutes | Serves 1

35g dairy-free chocolate, chopped
150ml dairy-free milk
50ml dairy-free cream
Dairy-free whipped cream (optional)

1. Place the chopped chocolate into your favourite mug or cup.
2. Pour the milk and cream into a saucepan and heat to boiling point. Immediately pour over the chopped chocolate and leave to sit for 2 minutes.
3. Stir well and then top with dairy-free whipped cream if desired.

Chocolate Ganache and Classic French Fruit Tarts

Free-From:

Prep time: 1 hour 15 minutes | Baking time: 15 minutes | Makes 1 x 20cm sweet pastry case

If I'm ever in a French patisserie, my choice is always a tarte aux fruits. Crisp sweet pastry, smooth vanilla pastry cream, topped with jewel-like glazed fruit... I think these tarts are utterly divine. But perhaps you prefer a rich chocolate ganache in contrast to the crisp sweet pastry? Either way, these are desserts with a wow factor. I tend to serve them on New Year's Eve, and I hope you enjoy them as much as we do.

For the sweet pastry case

140g plain flour
45g icing sugar
Pinch of salt
60g dairy-free butter, chilled and cubed
1 tbsp water
1 tsp vanilla extract

1. Place the flour, sugar and salt into a bowl. Rub in the cold, cubed butter until you have a mixture that resembles fine breadcrumbs.
2. Add the water and vanilla, then bring to a dough. Knead lightly until it's nice and smooth and then roll out between 2 sheets of parchment paper to a circle just larger than your 20cm tart tin or ring. Place the pastry in the fridge for at least 30 minutes to rest.
3. Roll out the chilled pastry a little more and then line the tin, making sure you push the pastry into the corners. Trim off the excess, prick the bottom with a fork and then chill again for at least 30 minutes.
4. Bake for 15 minutes at 165°c until lightly golden. Cool before removing from the tin.

Chocolate Ganache Tart

170g dairy-free chocolate, chopped
250ml dairy-free milk
45g sugar
1 tbsp cornflour
1 tsp vanilla extract
1 sweet pastry case (see above)

1. Place the chopped chocolate in a heatproof bowl.
2. Combine the milk, sugar, cornflour, and vanilla in a saucepan. Whisking the whole time, bring this mixture to the boil.
3. Once boiling, pour the milk mixture over the chopped chocolate and stir until smooth.
4. Pour the ganache into the pastry case and level off. Place in the fridge for at least an hour to fully set.

Classic French Fruit Tart

1 portion of crème pâtissière (see page 126)
1 sweet pastry case (see above)
Fruit of your choice, to cover
3 tbsp smooth apricot jam

1. Pipe an even layer of the pastry cream into the pastry case.
2. Decoratively place the fruit over the top so the cream is completely covered.
3. Melt the jam with 1 teaspoon of water. Once hot, brush this over the entire tart.

Suggested Combinations

Here are a few ways in which you may want to combine some of the recipes in this book for a special occasion.

A Children's Birthday Tea

Magic Mini Cupcakes (page 19)

Legendary Vegetarian Sausage Rolls (page 68)

Raspberry and Vanilla Pinwheel Cookies (page 82)

Perfect Chocolate Celebration Cake (page 84)

Caramel Crispy Bars, cut into small cubes (page 88)

Serve with finger sandwiches, vegetable batons and fruit

A Grown-Up Birthday Tea

Chocolate Truffles Two Ways (page 30)

Savoury Scones with Chive Butter (page 32)

Victoria Sponge Cake (page 60) or Perfect Chocolate Celebration Cake (page 84)

Classic French Fruit Tarts (page 130)

Serve with Champagne or sparkling elderflower

An Elegant Afternoon Tea

Victoria Sponge Cake (page 60)

Sensational Scones with Speedy Raspberry Jam (page 70)

The Best Ever Chocolate Cookies (page 92)

Mini Devil's Food Cakes (page 102)

Pomegranate Fruit Jellies (page 122)

Serve with your tea of choice in dainty cups and saucers

A Picnic

Pizza Breadsticks with Marinara Dip (page 44)

Fabulous Flapjacks with Two Twists (page 58)

Legendary Vegetarian Sausage Rolls (page 68)

Popcorn Cereal Bars (page 72)

You might also want to pack sandwiches (the whipped herby cream cheese on page 56 makes a lovely sandwich filling)

Brunch

Perfect Egg-Free Pancakes with Cherry Berry Compote (page 22)

Breakfast Cereal Cookies (page 26)

Crunchy Munchy Granola (page 54)

Marvellous Muffins (page 94)

A Christmas Party

Savoury Nibbles (page 108)

Mini Gingerbread Cookies (page 110)

Homemade Matchmakers and Peppermint Creams (page 112)

Christmas Cake (page 120) or Tiffin Wreath Cake (page 118)

An Easter Gathering

Homemade Easter Eggs (page 38)

Hot Cross Buns (page 36)

Lemon Sherbet Drizzle Cake (page 40)

A Drinks Party

Pizza Breadsticks with Marinara Dip (page 44)

Legendary Vegetarian Sausage Rolls (page 68)

Apple Galette, thinly sliced (page 78)

Savoury Nibbles (page 108)

Mocha Biscotti (page 128)

NOMO
MISSING OUT
CIOUSLY CREAMY
HOC BAR
Free From
EGG · NUTS
NOMO
NO MISSING OUT
DELICIOUSLY DARK
CHOCOLATE
Vegan & Free From
AIRY · GLUTEN · EGG · NUTS
85g
MISSING
DELICIOUSLY CREAMY
CHOC BAR
Vegan & Free From
DAIRY · GLUTEN · EGG · NUTS
85g

THE ORIGINAL
OATLY!
CREAMY OAT
Use as single cream
250 ml
THE ORIGINAL
OATLY!
whippable
CREAMY OAT
Use as double cream
CREAMY OAT SPREAD
PLAIN
150g
THE ORIGINAL
OATLY!
OATGURT
GREEK STYLE
400g
0.69
THE ORIGINAL
OAT-LY!
No milk.
No soy.
No ...eh...
whatever.
Totally vegan

Resources and Products – My Recommendations

Recommended reading for allergies

My Family & Food Allergies by Alexa Baracaia

Understanding Allergy by Dr Sophie Farooque

Living With Allergies by Emma Amoscato

You, Me and Food Allergies by Emma Amoscato

Anaphylaxis: The Essential Guide: An Action Plan for Living with Life-Threatening Allergies by Ruth Holroyd

Key websites relating to allergies

Natasha Allergy Research Foundation (www.narf.org.uk)

Allergy UK (www.allergyuk.org)

Anaphylaxis UK (www.anaphylaxis.org.uk)

Allergy Companions (www.allergycompanions.com – restaurant recommendations for those with dietary requirements)

The Allergy Collective (www.allergycollective.co.uk – a brilliant resource for building resilience for those with allergies)

Recommended brands

Remember that ingredients and production methods can change, so always check the label before use.

Milks – Oatly Original is our go-to oat milk. Make sure you buy the non-organic versions for dairy-free milks fortified with calcium.

Cheeses – Violife Original Slices have a pleasing mild cheesy flavour. Oatly Creamy Spread has a lovely mild taste and creamy consistency, making it an ideal cream cheese replacement. We also use Marigold or BOSH Nutritional Yeast.

Yoghurts – Alpro, Oatly Greek Style Oatgurt.

Creams – Oatly Creamy Oat and Whippable Creamy Oat creams are my preferred dairy-free replacements, giving great results with a lovely light creamy taste and texture. Violife and Alpro make good versions too. Food Heaven whipped cream in an aerosol can is great for adding a little pizazz to your puddings.

Butter and Margarine – Flora Plant Butter, Pure Sunflower

Chocolate – Nomo is my preferred chocolate brand, and most importantly it's entirely free-from milk, eggs, nuts and gluten. I find this chocolate not only delicious but high-quality and easy to temper, and it works superbly in all my recipes. I favour the dark bars for a richer taste, but the creamy ones work well too. Both Pacari and MooFree are also entirely free from milk and nuts. Callebaut NXT is a new allergen-free high quality chocolate made using tiger nuts (despite the name, tiger nuts are a legume not a nut).

Cocoa Powder - Sevenhills Organic, Asda own brand

Custard Powder - Just Whole Foods

Icing Sugar – Sainsbury's own brand, Sugar and Crumbs, Tate & Lyle

Fondant Icing – Beau Sugar Paste

Products to be cautious of – Always read the label

Chocolate – often may contain milk and nuts

Cocoa powder – sometimes may contain milk

Custard powder – sometimes may contain milk

Icing sugar – sometimes may contain egg

Fondant icing – sometimes may contain nuts

Dairy-free creams – some contain nuts, soya and/or coconut

Yoghurt – may contain nuts, soya, coconut

Seeds and dried fruit – may contain nuts

Stockists and sourcing ingredients

The major supermarkets all stock a variety of suitable free-from ingredients.

Nut-Free Marketplace – a treasure trove of nut-free goodies. The place to buy nut-free fondant icing.

The Vegan Kind – excellent online shop for plant-based creams and cheeses, chocolates and other groceries. Do be aware that the information on site may not fully show products that may contain traces of allergens.

Nomo – buy great chocolate directly from the manufacturers or from major supermarkets.

MooFree – great online shop with plenty of bargains and factory seconds available for a reduced price.

Acknowledgements

I would like to start by thanking my wonderful family: Dave, Sasha, and Sofia. You are my inspiration, the reason why this book exists, and your encouragement, enthusiasm, patience, love, and support made this process possible. I hope this book will make food a little bit brighter and sweeter for you, as well as for many others. I can't forget Luna, our dog, who has kept our sanity by providing mind-clearing walks, fluffy companionship, and a joyful wagging tail.

I would also like to thank my mother Judith, and brother James, for their love, support, constant encouragement and bringing creativity and colour into my life. And, Christiane, my mother-in-law, for being one of my most enthusiastic taste testers and putting up with many of the less successful experiments along the way!

Bringing this book to print has been a dream come true for me and would not have been possible without the wonderful team at Meze Publishing. Each step of the journey has been a joy, both enjoyable and straightforward.

Phil Turner for being onboard with the book from the offset and helping to hone the idea from a loose concept to the finished article.

Katie Fisher has made the editing process far easier and more enjoyable than I'd expected, and I have really enjoyed working with her.

Paul Cocker is a very talented designer and has helped bring my dream book to life.

Paul Gregory is without doubt an exceptional food photographer, has shown off the recipes to their best and has also been great fun to work with.

Emma Toogood and Lizzy Capps have excelled at marketing and PR.

Life with allergies is harder than it should be, and I'd like to thank all our friends and family who've made that extra effort, checked those ingredients, and even followed my recipes to make sure my girls haven't missed out. You are all exceptional people.

I would also like to thank the allergy community; you may not think a group of people who've bonded over food allergies on various online platforms would be a real community, but the allergy family is just that. Through Twitter Allergy Hour and various pages, groups and chats you have made this journey much easier and much more fun than it could have been.

But at the end of the day this book is for Sasha and Sofia, and for everyone else out there who needs or wants to think twice before eating something. If this book makes it a bit easier for you to have delicious things to eat, that you can share with those around you and that everyone can equally enjoy, then I have achieved my objective. Happy Friendly Baking!

Recipes by Category

Biscuits and Cookies

Breakfast

Buns and Breads

Cakes

Chocolate

Drinks

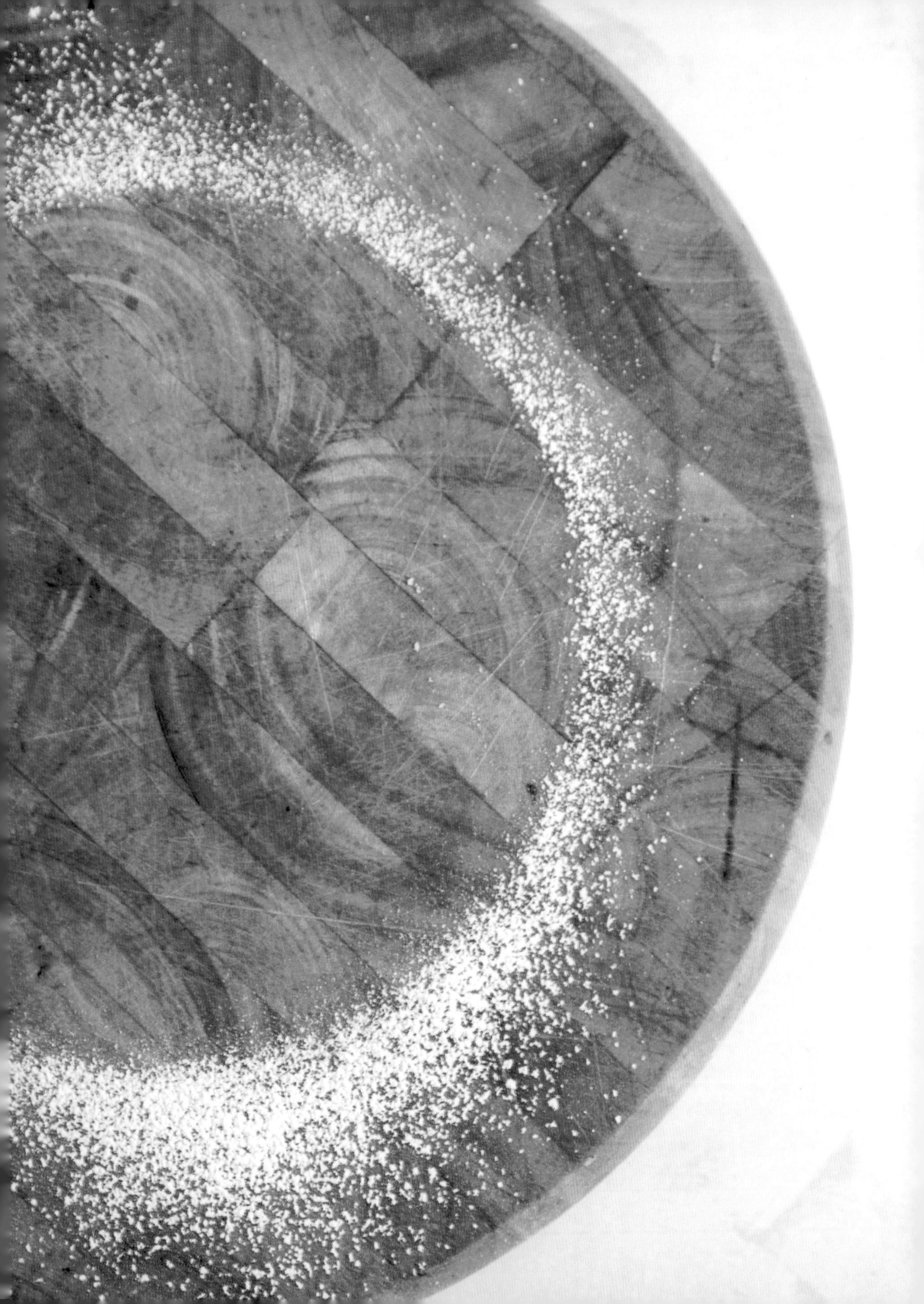